# A LIFE FOR GOD

W9-CGL-119

# A LIFE FOR GOD
## *The Mother Teresa Reader*

Compiled by LaVonne Neff

Servant Publications
Ann Arbor, Michigan

© 1995 by Servant Publications
All rights reserved.

Charis Books is an imprint of Servant Publications especially designed to serve Roman Catholics.

Scripture texts used in this work, unless otherwise indicated, are taken from *The New American Bible* (copyright 1970 by the Confraternity of Christian Doctrine, Washington, D.C. All rights reserved.) Selected texts are taken from the Revised Standard Version of the Bible (RSV), copyrighted 1946, 1952, 1971 by the Division of Christian Education of the National Council of Churches of Christ in the USA. Used by permission. Some Scripture quotations are taken from the King James Version of the Bible (KJV), or are Mother Teresa's own paraphrases.

Material from the following resources was used in the compilation of this volume with the permission of the publisher: *Jesus: The Word to Be Spoken, Total Surrender, Heart of Joy, Loving Jesus, One Heart Full of Love,* and *Suffering Into Joy.* All rights reserved.

Published by Servant Publications
P.O. Box 8617
Ann Arbor, Michigan 48107

Cover photograph: UPI/Bettman
Cover design by Diane Bareis

95 96 97 98 99 10 9 8 7 6 5 4 3 2 1

Printed in the United States of America
ISBN 0-89283-900-7

**Library of Congress Cataloging-in-Publication Data**

A life for God : the Mother Teresa reader / compiled by LaVonne Neff.

p. cm.

"Charis books."

ISBN 0-89283-900-7

1. Spiritual life—Catholic Church. 2. Catholic Church—Membership. I. Teresa, Mother, 1910- . II. Neff, LaVonne.

BX2350.2.L48 1995

248.4'82—dc20 95-9014

CIP

# EPIGRAPH

O Jesus,
you who suffer,
grant that, today and every day,
I may be able to see you in the person of your sick ones
and that, by offering them my care,
I may serve you.
Grant that, even if you are hidden under the unattractive disguise of
anger, of crime, or of madness,
I may recognize you and say,
"Jesus, you who suffer, how sweet it is to serve you."

Give me, Lord, this vision of faith,
and my work will never be monotonous,
I will find joy in harboring the small whims and desires
of all the poor who suffer.
Dear sick one, you are still more beloved to me
because you represent Christ.
What a privilege I am granted in being able to take care of you!

O God, since you are Jesus who suffers,
deign to be for me also
a Jesus who is patient, indulgent with my faults,
who looks only at my intentions,
which are to love you and to serve you
in the person of each of these children of yours who suffer.
Lord, increase my faith.
Bless my efforts and my work,
now and forever.

Mother Teresa of Calcutta

# CONTENTS

# PART ONE

## *Mother Teresa: A Soul of Prayer*

*Orare est laborare; laborare est orare.* "To pray is to work; to work is to pray." This ancient Benedictine motto could also be Mother Teresa's. Known around the world for her work as a servant to the poorest of the poor, she bathes her work in daily, constant prayer.

Some of her prayer is spoken: favorite prayers that she says daily, at Mass, and in group devotions. Some of her prayer is silent: the wordless contemplation of God in the quiet of the chapel every evening or in the faces of the poor she meets by day. Mother Teresa often tells people that continual prayer is what makes the difference between Missionaries of Charity and social workers. "We are contemplatives," she says of her order, "in the heart of the world."

Part One is an introduction to Mother Teresa's life and work, all set in the context of prayer.

ONE

# *A Contemplative in the Heart of the World*

Listen to Mother Teresa describe a typical day for the Missionaries of Charity in Calcutta:

• Our lives are centered on the Eucharist and prayer. We begin our day with Mass, Holy Communion, and meditation.

After Mass and breakfast, some sisters go to the home for dying destitutes, some to the leper colonies, some to the little schools we have in the slums, some take care of the preparation and distribution of food, some go visit needy families, some go teach catechism, and so on.

They go all over the city. (In Calcutta alone, we have fifty-nine centers. The home for dying destitutes is only one center.) The sisters travel everywhere with a rosary in hand. That is the way we pray in the streets. We do not go to the people without praying. The rosary has been our strength and our protection.

We always go in twos, and we come back around 12:30. At that time we have our lunch. After lunch, very often we have to do housework.

Then, for half an hour, every sister has to rest, because all the time they are on their feet. After that, we have an examination of conscience, pray the Liturgy of the Hours, and the Via Crucis, "Way of the Cross."

At 2:00, we have spiritual reading for half an hour, and then a cup of tea.

At 3:00, the professed sisters again go out. (Novices and postulants remain in the house. They have classes in theology and Scripture and other subjects, such as the rules of monastic orders.)

Between 6:15 and 6:30, everybody comes back home.

From 6:30 to 7:30, we have adoration of the Blessed Sacrament. To be able to have this hour of adoration, we have not had to cut back on our work. We can work as many as ten or even twelve hours a day in service to the poor following this schedule.

At 7:30, we have dinner.

After dinner, for about twenty minutes, we have to prepare the work for next morning.

From 8:30 until 9:00, we have recreation. Everybody talks at the top of her lungs, after having worked all day long.

At 9:00, we go to the chapel for night prayers and to prepare the meditations for the next morning.

Once a week, every week, we have a day of recollection. That day, the first-year novices go out, because they are the ones who don't go out every day. Then all the professed sisters stay in for the day of recollection. That day we also go to confession and spend more time in adoration of the Blessed Sacrament.

This is time when we can regain our strength and fill up our emptiness again with Jesus. That's why it is a very beautiful day.

*Pray without ceasing.* **1 Thessalonians 5:17 (KJV)**

• We must join our prayer with work. We try to bring this across to our sisters by inviting them to make their work a prayer. How is it possible to change one's work into a prayer? Work cannot substitute for prayer. Nevertheless, we can learn to make work a prayer. How can we do this? By doing our work with Jesus and for Jesus. That is the way to make our work a prayer. It is possible that I may not be able to keep my attention fully on God while I work, but God doesn't demand that I do so. Yet I can fully desire and intend that my work be done with Jesus and for Jesus. This is beautiful and that is what God wants. He wants our will and our desire to be for him, for our family, for our children, for our brethren, and for the poor.

• We begin our day by trying to see Christ through the eucharistic bread. Throughout the day we keep in touch with him under the appearances of the shattered bodies of our poor. In this way our work becomes a prayer, as we accomplish it with Jesus, for Jesus, and toward Jesus.

• The poor are our prayer. They carry God in themselves. Prayer is in all things, in all gestures.

• In reality, there is only one true prayer, only one substantial prayer: Christ himself. There is only one voice which rises above the face of the earth: the voice of Christ. The voice reunites and coordinates in itself all the voices raised in prayer.

• Pray lovingly like children, with an earnest desire to love much and to make loved the one that is not loved.

• Perfect prayer does not consist in many words but in the fervor of the desire which raised the heart to Jesus. Jesus has chosen us to be souls of prayer. The value of our actions corresponds exactly to the value of the prayer we make, and our actions are fruitful only if they are the true expression of earnest prayer. We must fix our gaze on Jesus, and if we work together with Jesus we will do much better. We get anxious and restless because we try to work alone, without Jesus.

• Unity is the fruit of prayer, of humility, of love. Therefore, if the community prays together, it will stay together, and if you stay together you will love one another as Jesus loves each one of you. A real change of heart will make it really one heart full of love. This one heart our community offers to Jesus and to Our Lady, his mother.

• Love to pray, feel the need to pray often during the day, and take the trouble to pray. If you want to pray better, you must pray more. Prayer enlarges the heart until it is capable of containing God's gift of himself. Ask and seek, and your heart will grow big enough to receive him and keep him as your own.

• We want so much to pray properly and then we fail. We get discouraged and give up prayer. God allows the failure but he does not want the discouragement. He wants us to be more childlike, more humble, more grateful in prayer, and not to try to pray alone, as we all belong to the mystical body of Christ, which is praying always. There is always prayer; there is no such thing as "I pray," but Jesus in me and Jesus with me prays; therefore the body of Christ prays.

• To pray generously is not enough; we must pray devoutly, with fervor and piety. We must pray perseveringly and with great love.

• Our prayers are mostly vocal prayers; they should be burning words coming forth from the furnace of a heart filled with love. In these prayers, speak to God with great reverence and confidence.... Do not drag or run ahead; do not shout or keep silent but devoutly, with great sweetness, with natural simplicity, without any affectation, offer your praise to God with the whole of your heart and soul. We must know the meaning of the prayers we say and feel the sweetness of each word to make these prayers of great profit; we must sometimes meditate on them and often during the day find our rest in them.

• The prayer that comes from the mind and heart and which we do not read in books is called mental prayer. We must never forget that we are bound by our state to tend toward perfection and to aim ceaselessly at it. The practice of daily mental prayer is necessary to reach our goal. Because it is the breath of life to our soul, holiness is impossible without it. St. Teresa of Avila says, "She who gives up mental prayer does not require the devil to push her into hell; she goes there of her own accord." It is only by mental prayer and spiritual reading that we can cultivate the gift of prayer. Mental prayer is greatly fostered by simplicity—that is, forgetfulness of self by mortifications of the body and of our senses, and by frequent aspirations which feed our prayer. "In mental prayer," says St. John Vianney, "shut your eyes, shut your mouth, and open your heart." In vocal prayer we speak to God, in mental prayer he speaks to us. It is then that God pours himself into us.

• Let us improve our spirit of prayer and recollection. Let us free our minds from all that is not Jesus. If you find it difficult to pray, ask him again and again, "Jesus, come into my heart, pray in me and with me, that I may learn from thee how to pray." If you pray more you will pray better. Take the help of all your senses to pray.

• We should be professionals in prayer. The apostles understood this very well. When they saw that they might be lost in a multitude of works, they decided to give themselves to continual prayer and to the ministry of the Word. We have to pray on behalf of those who do not pray.

• For us religious, prayer is a sacred duty and sublime mission. Conscious of the many urgent needs and interests we carry in our hands, we will ascend the altar of prayer, take up our rosary, turn to all the other spiritual exercises with great longing, and go with confidence to the throne of grace, that we may obtain mercy and find grace and seasonable aid for ourselves and our souls.

• People are hungry for the Word of God that will give peace, that will give unity, that will give joy. But you cannot give what you don't have. That's why it is necessary to deepen your life of prayer. Allow Jesus to take you, pray with you and through you, and then you will be a real, true contemplative in the heart of the world.

• We shall make use of our gestures and postures in prayer to grow in the depth of prayer and contemplation of God by using them meaningfully and with devotion. Therefore, we shall—

- —use the holy water with devotion as a sign of interior cleansing and blessing of God;
- —make the sign of the cross beautifully as a sign of belonging entirely to the Father, Son, and Holy Spirit, set aside totally for contemplation and love, sealed against the powers of the flesh, world, and the devil;
- —keep our hands joined in prayer as a sign of deep reverence and adoration of God;

— kneel and genuflect with devotion as a sign of adoration, supplication, intercession, humility, and penance;
— pray standing straight in liturgical prayer as a sign of our community participation of the people of God in the public worship of the church—the pilgrim church on the way to the Father—our liberation and resurrection in Christ, and of our respect, alertness, and readiness for anything;
— pray sitting with deep recollection as a sign of listening, docility, intimacy, contemplation, and loving trust;
— bow low in adoration as a sign of total surrender.

• We shall do our utmost to introduce and encourage personal and family prayer, meditation and prayerful reading, and if possible sharing the Word of God in the Scriptures in every home we visit.

• Sometimes we do not get from prayer what we are seeking because we do not focus our attention and our heart on Christ, through whom our prayers reach God. Often a deep and fervent look at Christ is the best prayer: I look at him and he looks at me.

• Our prayers should be delicious and hot victuals that come from the fire of a heart overflowing with love.

• If we want to be able to love, we must pray! Prayer will give us a clean heart, and a clean heart can see God. If we see God, immediately God's love works in us. And we need to love not with words, but with deeds!

• When we look at the cross, we discover how much Jesus loved us. When we look at the tabernacle, we know how much he loves us now. That is why it is very important for us, if we really want to love and to be loved, to learn to pray. Let us teach our children to pray. Let's pray with them.

• Think of the fruit of our prayer:
The fruit of prayer is faith. Prayer leads us to say: "I believe."

The fruit of faith is love. Faith leads us to say: "I love." The fruit of love is service. Love leads us to say: "I want to serve."

And the fruit of service is peace.

• Someone asked me what advice I had for politicians. I don't like to get involved in politics, but my answer just popped out, "They should spend time on their knees. I think that would help them to become better statesmen."

• Every time we need to make a decision concerning our families, we need to pray. Jesus said, "Ask and you will receive. Seek and you will find. Knock and the door will be opened" (Lk 11:9). Nothing will be denied you. Our congregation [in Calcutta] is living proof of that. We are now more than a thousand. Thousands of lives depend on us. In spite of that, we have never, never, never had to say to anybody, "Go away. We can't do anything for you." God is always there showing us that he never leaves our prayers unanswered. And to confirm this, since we are more important than the lilies of the field, God always helps us.

• I don't think there is anyone who needs God's help and grace as much as I do. Sometimes I feel so helpless and weak. I think that is why God uses me. Because I cannot depend on my own strength, I rely on him twenty-four hours a day. If the day had even more hours, then I would need his help and grace during those hours as well. All of us must cling to God through prayer and sacrifice.

**Q:** *You love people that others consider the rejects of humanity. What is the secret that allows you to do this?*

**A:** My secret is very simple: I pray. Through prayer I become one in love with Christ. I realize that praying to him is loving him. That means that I am fulfilling his commandment. Let's not forget what he tells us: "I was hungry and you fed me not" (see Matthew 25:42). The poor who live in the slums of the world are the suffering Christ. The Son of God lives and dies through them, and through them

God shows me his true face. For me, prayer means being united to the will of God twenty-four hours a day, to live for him, through him, and with him.

• The fruit of our work, as well as the ability to carry it out, comes from prayer. The work that we accomplish is the fruit of our union with Christ. We have been called to give Jesus to the peoples of the world, so that they can look at him and discover his love, his compassion, and his humility in action.

• Jesus is our prayer, and he is also the answer to all our prayer. He has chosen to be himself in us the living song of love, praise, adoration, thanksgiving, intercession and reparation to the Father in the name of the whole creation, especially the poorest of the poor and those who do not pray, who do not know how to pray, who do not dare and do not want to pray.

• Singing is an important part of our life of prayer. We shall keep our singing simple and use a minimum of musical instruments when necessary.

• Jesus Christ has told us that we ought "always to pray and not to faint" (Lk 18:1). St. Paul says, "pray without ceasing" (1 Thes 5:17). God calls all men and women to this disposition of heart—to pray always. Let the love of God once take entire and absolute possession of a heart; let it become to that heart like a second nature; let that heart suffer nothing contrary to enter; let it apply itself continually to increase this love of God by seeking to please him in all things and refusing him nothing; let it accept as from his hand everything that happens to it; let it have a firm determination never to commit any fault deliberately and knowingly or, if it should fail, to be humbled and to rise up again at once, and such a heart will pray continually.

• People today speak much about the poor, but they do not know or talk to the poor. So, too, we can talk much about prayer and yet not know how to pray.

• Does your mind and your heart go to Jesus as soon as you get up in the morning? This is prayer, that you turn your mind and heart to God. In your times of difficulties, in sorrows, in sufferings, in temptations, and in all things, where did your mind and heart turn first of all? How did you pray? Did you take the trouble to turn to Jesus and pray, or did you seek consolations?

Has your faith grown? If you do not pray, your faith will leave you.

Ask the Holy Spirit to pray in you. Learn to pray, love to pray, and pray often. Feel the need to pray and to want to pray.

If you have learned how to pray, then I am not afraid for you. If you know how to pray, then you will love prayer—and if you love to pray, then you will pray. Knowledge will lead to love and love to service.

• If you don't pray, your presence will have no power, your words will have no power. If you pray, you will be able to overcome all the tricks of the devil. Don't believe all the thoughts that he puts into your mind.

• Prayer enlarges the heart until it is capable of containing God's gift of himself. Ask and seek and your heart will grow big enough to receive him and keep him as your own.

• Be sincere in your prayers. Do you know how to pray? Do you love to pray? Sincerity is nothing but humility, and you acquire humility only by accepting humiliations. All that has been said about humility is not enough to teach you humility. All that you have read about humility is not enough to teach you humility. You learn humility only by accepting humiliations. And you will meet humiliation all through your lives.

The greatest humiliation is to know that you are nothing. This you come to know when you face God in prayer. When you come face to face with God, you cannot but know that you are nothing, that you have nothing. In the silence of the heart God speaks. If you face God in prayer and silence, God will speak to you. Then you will know that you are nothing. It is only when you realize your nothingness, your emptiness, that God can fill you with himself.

When you become full of God, you will do all your work well, all of it wholeheartedly. We have our fourth vow of wholehearted service: it means to be full of God. And when you are full of God, you will do everything well. This you can do only if you pray, if you know how to pray, if you love prayer, and if you pray well.

• Prayer is the very life of oneness, of being one with Christ. Therefore, prayer is as necessary as the air, as the blood in our body, as anything to keep us alive—to keep us alive to the grace of God.

• It is impossible to engage in the apostolate without being a soul of prayer, without a conscious awareness of and submission to the divine will. We must be aware of our oneness with Christ, as he was aware of his oneness with his Father. Our activity is truly apostolic only insofar as we permit him to work in and through us—with his power, his desire, his love. We must become holy, not because we want to feel holy, but because Christ must be able to live his life fully in us.

• See how Jesus taught his disciples to pray: Call God your Father; praise and glorify his name; do his will as the saints do it in heaven; ask for daily bread, spiritual and temporal; ask for forgiveness of your own sins and for the grace to forgive others; ask for the grace to resist temptations and for the final grace to be delivered from the evil which is in you and around you.

• Failure and loss of vocation also come from neglect of prayer. As prayer is the food of spiritual life, neglect of prayer starves the spiritual life and loss of vocation is unavoidable. Let us ask Our Lady in our own simple way to teach us how to pray, as she taught Jesus in all the years that he was with her in Nazareth.

• You should make all effort to walk in the presence of God, to see God in all persons you meet, to live out your morning meditation throughout the day. When you go out for your task, spread all around you the joy of belonging to God, of living with God, of being his own. In the streets, in the poor neighborhoods, at work, pray always with all your heart and all your soul. Keep the silence which Jesus kept throughout thirty years of life in Nazareth and which he continues to keep today in the tabernacle, interceding for us. Pray as Mary did, for she kept all things in her heart, through prayer and meditation, and she continues to be a mediatrix of all graces.

• Pray. Ask for the necessary grace. Pray to be able to understand how much Jesus loved us, so that you can love others. And pray for the sisters, that we won't spoil God's work. Pray that we allow Jesus to use each of us as he wishes and wherever he wishes.

*For God alone my soul waits in silence;*
*from him comes my salvation.* **Psalm 62:1 (RSV)**

• Souls of prayer are souls of great silence.

• There is a very important theologian, a very holy priest, who is also one of the best in India right now. I know him very well, and I said to him, "Father, you talk all day about God. How close you must be to God! You are talking all the time about God." And you know what he said to me? He said, "I may be talking much about God, but I may be talking very little to God." And then he explained, "I may be rattling off so many words and may be saying many good things, but deep down I have not got the time to listen. Because in the silence of the heart, God speaks."

• It is difficult to pray if you don't know how to pray, but we must help ourselves to pray. The first means to use is silence. We cannot put ourselves directly in the presence of God if we do not practice internal and external silence. Therefore we shall take as a special point silence of mind, eyes, and tongue.

• Silence gives us a new outlook on everything. We need silence to be able to touch souls. The essential thing is not what we say but what God says to us and through us. Jesus is always waiting for us in silence. In that silence, he will listen to us, there he will speak to our soul, and there we will hear his voice.

• The contemplative aspect of our missionary call makes us gather the whole universe and bring it to the very center of our heart, where he who is the source and the Lord of the universe abides, and remain in communion with him, drinking deeply from the very source the deep calm and peace of interior quietude and refreshment of God, allowing the pure water of divine grace to flow plentifully and unceasingly from the source itself on to the whole of his creation.

• The interior silence is very difficult, but we must make the effort to pray. In silence we will find new energy and true unity. The energy of God will be ours to do all things well, and so will the unity of our thoughts with his thoughts, the unity of our prayers with his prayers, the unity of our actions with his actions, of our life with his life. All our words will be useless unless they come from within. Words which do not give the light of Christ increase the darkness.

• This is what we have to learn right from the beginning, to listen to the voice of God in our heart, and then in the silence of the heart God speaks. Then from the fullness of our hearts, our mouth will have to speak. That is the connection.

In the silence of the heart, God speaks and you have to listen. Then in the fullness of your heart, because it is full of God, full of love, full of compassion, full of faith, your mouth will speak.

Listen in silence, because if your heart is full of other things you cannot hear the voice of God. But when you have listened to the voice of God in the stillness of your heart, then your heart is filled with God, like Our Lady full of grace. And then from the fullness of the heart the mouth will speak.

This will need much sacrifice, but if we really mean to pray and want to pray we must be ready to do it now. These are only the first steps toward prayer but if we never make the first step with a determination, we will not reach the last one: the presence of God.

• Before you speak, it is necessary for you to listen, for God speaks in the silence of the heart. You have to listen, and only then, from the fullness of your heart, you speak and God listens.

• The contemplatives and ascetics of all ages and religions have sought God in the silence and solitude of the desert, forest, and mountain. Jesus himself spent forty days in the desert and long hours in communing with the Father in the silence of the night on the mountains.

• We too are called to withdraw at certain intervals into deeper silence and aloneness with God, together as a community as well as personally, to be alone with him, not with our books, thoughts, and memories but completely stripped of everything, to dwell lovingly in his presence: silent, empty, expectant, and motionless.

• God is a friend of silence. We cannot find him in noise or agitation. Nature—trees, flowers, grass—grows in silence. The stars, the moon, and the sun move in silence.

The apostles say, "We will devote ourselves to prayer and to the ministry of the word" (Acts 6:4, RSV). The more we receive in our silent prayer, the more we will be able to give in our active life. Silence gives us a new vision of things. We need that silence in order to get through to souls. What is essential is not what we say but what God tells us and what he tells others through us.

Jesus always waits for us in silence. In silence he listens to us; in silence he speaks to our souls. In silence we are granted the privilege of listening to his voice.

• It is difficult to pray if you don't know how to do it. We need to help each other in prayers.

• Each one of us will take it as our serious and sacred duty to collaborate with one another in our common effort to promote and maintain an atmosphere of deep silence and recollection in our own lives, conducive to the constant awareness of the Divine Presence everywhere and in everyone, especially in our own hearts and in the hearts of our sisters with whom we live in the poorest of the poor.

• Silence of the tongue will teach us so much: to speak to Christ, to be joyful at recreation, and to have many things to say. At recreation Christ speaks to us through others and at meditation he speaks to us directly. Silence also makes us so much more Christlike because he had a special love for this virtue.

• Then we have the silence of the eyes which will always help us to see God. Our eyes are like two windows through which Christ or the world comes to our hearts. Often we need great courage to keep them closed. How often we say, "I wish I had not seen this thing," and yet we take so little trouble to overcome the desire to see everything.

• To make possible true interior silence, we shall practice:
- — *Silence of the eyes,* by seeking always the beauty and goodness of God everywhere, closing them to the faults of others and to all that is sinful and disturbing to the soul;
- — *Silence of the ears,* by listening always to the voice of God and to the cry of the poor and the needy, closing them to all other voices that come from the evil one or from fallen human nature: e.g., gossip, tale-bearing, and uncharitable words;
- — *Silence of the tongue,* by praising God and speaking the life-giving Word of God that is the Truth that enlightens and inspires, brings peace, hope, and joy, and by refraining from self-defense and every word that causes darkness, turmoil, pain, and death;
- — *Silence of the mind,* by opening it to the truth and knowledge of God in prayer and contemplation, like Mary who pondered the marvels of the Lord in her heart, and by closing it to all untruths, distractions, destructive thoughts, rash judgment, false suspicions of others, revengeful thoughts, and desires;

— *Silence of the heart*, by loving God with our whole heart, soul, mind, and strength and one another as God loves, desiring God alone and avoiding all selfishness, hatred, envy, jealousy, and greed.

• Our silence is a joyful and God-centered silence; it demands of us constant self-denial and plunges us into the deep silence of God where aloneness with God becomes a reality.

• To foster and maintain a prayerful atmosphere of exterior silence we shall—

— respect certain times and places of more strict silence;
— move about and work prayerfully, quietly, and gently;
— avoid at all costs all unnecessary speaking and notice;
— speak, when we have to, softly, gently, saying just what is necessary;
— look forward to profound silence as a holy and precious time, a withdrawal into the living silence of God.

• Regarding purity, Jesus said, "Blessed are the clean of heart, for they shall see God" (see Matthew 5:8). If our hearts are filled with uncharitableness and jealousy, we cannot see God. I can spend hours in church, but I will not see God if my heart is not pure. That is why we need silence. In the silence and purity of the heart God speaks.

• Silence of our eyes.
Silence of our ears.
Silence of our mouths.
Silence of our minds.
Silence of our hearts.
For in the silence of the heart God will speak. Give Jesus these five silences as a token of your gratitude.

• You will never learn to pray until you keep silence:
The fruit of silence is faith.
The fruit of faith is prayer.

The fruit of prayer is love.
The fruit of love is service.
And the fruit of service is silence.

• Silence of the heart, not only of the mouth—that too is necessary. Then you can hear God everywhere: in the closing of the door, in the person who needs you, in the birds that sing, in the flowers, the animals—that silence which is wonder and praise. Why? Because God is everywhere, and you can see and hear him. That crow is praising God. That stupid crow—I can hear it well. We can see and hear God in that crow, but we cannot see and hear him if our heart is not clean.

• Jesus spent forty days before beginning his public life in silence. He often retired alone to spend the night on the mountain in silence and prayer. He who spoke with authority spent his early life in silence.

• See how nature, the trees, the flowers, and the grass grow in perfect silence. See the stars, the moon, and the sun, how they move in silence. The apostles said, "We will give ourselves continually at prayer and to the ministry of the Word" (see Acts 6:4). For the more we receive in silent prayer, the more we can give in our active life.

• If we are careful of silence it will be easy to pray and to pray fervently. There is so much talk, so much repetition, so much carrying of tales in words and in writing. Our prayer life suffers so much because our hearts are not silent.

*All of us, gazing on the Lord's glory with unveiled faces, are being transformed from glory to glory into his very image by the Lord who is the Spirit.* **2 Corinthians 3:18**

• Our contemplation is pure joy in our awareness of the presence of the Lord. It is pure silence in our experience of his fullness. Our contemplation is our life. It is not a matter of doing but being. It is the possession of our spirit by the Holy Spirit breathing into us the plentitude of God and sending us forth to the whole creation as his personal message of love.

• We shall not waste our time in looking for extraordinary experiences in our life of contemplation but live by pure faith, ever watchful and ready for his coming by doing our day-to-day duties with extraordinary love and devotion.

• Our life of contemplation is simply—
 — to realize God's constant presence and his tender love for us in the least little things of life;
 — to be constantly available to him, loving him with our whole heart, whole mind, whole soul, and whole strength, no matter in what form he may come to us.

• We are called to remain immersed in the contemplation of the Father, Son, and the Holy Spirit in their love for one another as well as in their love for us manifested in the great marvels of creation, redemption, and sanctification.

• We shall not rely much on books written by men to learn how to contemplate but place ourselves before Jesus and ask him to send us his Spirit to teach us how to contemplate.

• Jesus who contemplates in us is also the rock of our contemplation, our forest of meditation, desert of solitude, our hermitage and cave in whom we enter to remain deep in contemplation of God in communion with all our brothers and sisters.

• St. Thomas Aquinas says, "Those who have been called to action would be wrong to think that they are dispensed of contemplative life. Both tasks go closely together. Thus, these two lives, far from being mutually exclusive, involve one another, carrying with them the same means and helps and being mutually complemented. If action is to be fruitful, it needs contemplative life. And the latter, when it reaches a given degree of intensity, spreads part of its surplus over the first."

• As a contemplative, your mouth must be very pure to be able to utter those words of God all the time, just as our hands in our active life must be very pure when we touch the body of Christ. This is something that must be the very life of our life. Otherwise we could rattle off many things, and learn many things by heart, and know all possible knowledge, and all of theology and all the things about God, but we would not be able to light that fire in the hearts of the people. We are just uttering words, not living those words. That is why it is necessary for us that our words be the fruit of our life, the fruit of our prayers, the fruit of our penance, and the fruit of our adoration.

• We are called to love the world. And God loved the world so much that he gave Jesus. Today he loves the world so much that he gives you and me to be his love, his compassion, and that presence, that life of prayer, of sacrifice, of surrender to God. The response that God asks of you is to be a contemplative. Actually, every single Christian, every Catholic who lives a life united in the Eucharist, united with Jesus—he is the contemplative, she is the contemplative.

• If we take Jesus at his word, all of us are contemplatives in the heart of the world, for if we have faith, we are continually in his presence. We need a life of prayer to have this kind of faith. We need to worship God and have a spirit of sacrifice. We need to spiritually feed ourselves on him constantly.

• We are called to be contemplatives in the heart of the world by—
- —seeking the face of God in everything, everyone, everywhere, all the time, and his hand in every happening;
- —seeing and adoring the presence of Jesus, especially in the lowly appearance of bread, and in the distressing disguise of the poor, by praying the work, that is, by doing it with Jesus, for Jesus, and to Jesus.

• Our life of contemplation shall retain the following characteristics:

Missionary: by going out physically or in spirit in search of souls all over the world.

Contemplative: by gathering the whole world at the very center of our hearts where the Lord abides, and allowing the pure water of divine grace to flow plentifully and unceasingly from the source itself, on the whole of his creation.

Universal: by praying and contemplating with all and for all, especially with and for the spiritually poorest of the poor.

• Our lives must be connected with the living Christ in us. If we do not live in the presence of God, we cannot go on.

• The true interior life makes the active life burn forth and consume everything. It makes us find Jesus in the dark holes of the slums, in the most pitiful miseries of the poor—the God-Man naked on the cross, mournful, despised by all, the man of suffering crushed like a worm by the scourging and the crucifixion. This interior life motivates the Missionary of Charity to serve Jesus in the poor.

• I insist on saying that we are not social workers. We are really contemplatives in the heart of the world.

• By contemplation the soul draws directly from the heart of God the graces which the active life must distribute.

• Our active brothers and sisters put their service into action, and contemplative brothers and sisters put that loving action into prayer, into penance, into adoration, into contemplation, and into the proclamation of the Word that they have meditated on and adored. Active and contemplative are not two different lives; it is only that one is faith in action through service, the other faith in action through prayer.

• The Missionaries of Charity take literally the words of Jesus: "I was hungry, I was naked, without a home, and you gave me food, you clothed me, you gave me shelter" (see Matthew 25:35-36). In this way we are in contact with him twenty-four hours a day. This contemplation, this touching of Christ in the poor, is beautiful, very real, and full of love.

• Christ will not deceive us. That is why our lives must be woven around the Eucharist. The Christ who gives of himself to us under the appearance of bread and the Christ who is hidden under the distressing disguise of the poor, is the same Jesus.

• The poor are a gift that God bestows on us. But they need our life of prayer and our oneness with God. Real prayer is union with God, a union as vital as that of the vine and the branches, which is the illustration Jesus gives us in the Gospel of John. We need prayer. We need that union to produce good fruit. The fruit is what we produce with our hands, whether it be food, clothing, money, or something else. All of that is the fruit of our oneness with God. We need a life of prayer, of poverty, and of sacrifice to do this with love.

• Sacrifice and prayer complement each other. There is no prayer without sacrifice, and there is no sacrifice without prayer. That is what Jesus has shown us. Jesus' life was spent in intimate union with his Father as he passed through this world doing good. We need to do the same. Let's walk by his side. We need to give Christ a chance to make use of us to be his word and his work—to share his food and his clothing in the world today. If we do not radiate the light of Christ around us, the sense of the darkness that prevails in the world will increase. The people around us should be able to recognize him by our union with God.

• We must cleave to Jesus. Our whole life must simply be woven into Jesus. Jesus in the Mass, Jesus in my sisters, in the poor, at adoration. It is the same Jesus. Just as the wine and the grape are one; just as the branch fits so tightly into the vine—so we must be completely one with Jesus.

• Just as the seed is meant to be a tree—we are meant to grow into Jesus.

• If we neglect prayer and if the branch is not connected with the vine, it will die. That connecting of the branch to the vine is prayer. If that connection is there then love is there, then joy is there, and we will be the sunshine of God's love, the hope of eternal happiness, the flame of burning love. Why? Because we are one with Jesus. If you sincerely want to learn to pray: keep silence.

TWO

# *Her Life: A Biographical Sketch*

Born in southeastern Europe in 1910, Agnes Gonxha Bojaxhiu (Mother Teresa) grew to become a tiny nun among the destitute masses of the Calcutta slums. In time, her work grew to span the globe, causing her to become one of the best known and most highly respected women in the world. Winner of many awards, including the Nobel Peace Prize and the Templeton Award for Progress in Religion, she is personally acquainted with popes, presidents, and royalty. She has never hesitated, however, to do the most menial tasks, and one of her oft-repeated themes is the need for humility. Today there are over 4,000 religious sisters and brothers internationally in the 107 houses founded by the Missionaries of Charity.

The psalmist's description of God's loyal followers fits Mother Teresa:

> They that are planted in the house of the Lord
> shall flourish in the courts of our God.
> They shall bear fruit even in old age;
> vigorous and sturdy shall they be,
> Declaring how just is the Lord,
> my Rock, in whom there is no wrong.
>
> Psalm 92:14-16

*August 16, 1910: A daughter is born to the Bojaxhiu family.* The child who will one day be known as Mother Teresa is born in Skopje, capital of the Albanian republic of Macedonia. She is the third and last child of Nikolle Bojaxhiu and Drana Bernai, married in 1900. Her sister, Aga, was born in 1905 and her brother, Lazar, was born in 1907.

*August 27, 1910: She is baptized.* The child is baptized in the parish church of the Sacred Heart of Jesus and given the name Gonxha (Agnes). Her parents are very devout Catholics, especially her mother.

*1919: Her father dies.* Nikolle Bojaxhiu dies of an apparent poisoning after attending a political meeting. He was a municipal councilman with strong nationalist convictions.

*1915-24: Agnes has a happy childhood.* Along with her brother and her sister, Agnes attends public school. She does well, even though her health is somewhat delicate. She also attends catechism classes at the parish, joins the parish choir, and belongs to a Catholic youth organization called the "Daughters of Mary." She has special interest in reading about missionaries and the lives of the saints.

Mother Teresa sums up her family life during her childhood and adolescence: "We were all very united, especially after the death of my father. We lived for each other and we made every effort to make one another happy. We were a very united and a very happy family."

Lazar, the only son, commented about the religious life of his mother and sisters: "We lived next to the parish church of the Sacred Heart of Jesus. Sometimes my mother and sisters seemed to live as much in the church as they did at home. They were always involved with the choir, the religious services, and missionary topics."

Lazar also commented about his mother's generosity: "She never allowed any of the many poor people who came to our door to leave empty handed. When we would look at her strangely, she would say, 'Keep in mind that even those who are not our blood relatives, even if they are poor, are still our brethren.'"

At the age of twelve, Agnes feels her first gentle calling to the religious and missionary life, a calling that will lie dormant for several years. Meanwhile, she continues being an active member of the

Daughters of Mary. With the encouragement of her parish priests, who are Jesuits, she grows in her interest in missionary outreach. Agnes' brother, Lazar, moves to Austria to study at a military academy to become a cavalry officer.

*1928: Agnes joins the Sisters of Our Lady of Loreto.* Agnes' interest in missionary outreach is confirmed by a clear calling to the religious life while she is praying before the altar of the Patroness of Skopje: "Our Lady interceded for me and helped me to discover my vocation." With the guidance and help of a Yugoslav Jesuit, Agnes applies for admission to the Order of the Sisters of Our Lady of Loreto (commonly called the Irish Ladies), founded in the sixteenth century by Mary Ward. She is attracted by their missionary work in India.

*September 26, 1928: She travels to the motherhouse in Ireland.* Admitted provisionally, Agnes sets out on her trip to Dublin, traveling by train through Yugoslavia, Austria, Switzerland, France, and England until she arrives at the motherhouse of the Sisters of Our Lady of Loreto.

*December 1, 1928: She arrives in India.* After two months of intensive English language studies, Agnes sets out by ship for India, where she arrives on January 6, 1929, after thirty-seven days. Agnes stays in Calcutta only one week, after which she is sent to Darjeeling, in the foothills of the Himalayas, to begin her novitiate.

*May 24, 1931: Agnes becomes Sister Teresa.* After two years as a novice, Agnes professes temporary vows as a Sister of Our Lady of Loreto, changing her baptismal name for Teresa. "I chose the name Teresa for my religious vows. But it wasn't the name of the great Teresa of Avila. I chose the name of Teresa of the Little Flower, Thérèse of Lisieux."

*1930-37: Sister Teresa moves to Calcutta.* After professing her temporary vows, Sister Teresa lives in Calcutta and serves as a geography and history teacher at St. Mary's School, run by the Sisters of Our Lady of Loreto.

*May 24, 1937: Sister Teresa professes her final vows.* After renewing her temporary vows several times, Sister Teresa professes her final vows as a Sister of Our Lady of Loreto. Mother Teresa sums up very well her life in the religious order: "I was the happiest nun at Loreto. I dedicated myself to teaching. That job, carried out for the love of God, was a true apostolate. I liked it very much." She becomes the director of studies at St. Mary's.

*September 10, 1946: God calls her to serve the poor.* Mother Teresa calls it "a day of inspiration." She says, "While I was going by train from Calcutta to Darjeeling to participate in spiritual exercises, I was quietly praying when I clearly felt a call within my calling. The message was very clear. I had to leave the convent and consecrate myself to helping the poor by living among them. It was a command. I knew where I had to go, but I did not know how to get there."

*August 16, 1948: Rome gives her permission to pursue her new calling.* Leaving the Sisters of Our Lady of Loreto is difficult and painful for Sister Teresa. To do so, she needs special permission from Rome after an agreement is reached within her religious order. Finally, the permission is granted for her to live as a nun outside of the convent. She leaves on August 16, 1948, after taking off the religious habit of the Sisters of Our Lady of Loreto and putting on a white sari that looks like the ones worn by the poorest women in India. The sari has a blue border symbolizing her desire to imitate the Virgin Mary.

Mother Teresa leaves Calcutta to take an accelerated three-month course in basic nursing, then returns to put into practice her desire to dedicate herself to serving the poorest of the poor in the slums of Calcutta. This year she also applies for and is granted lifelong Indian citizenship. Pope Paul VI also grants her Vatican citizenship in the late 1970s to facilitate her missionary travels.

*March 19, 1949: The first follower joins Mother Teresa.* Subashini Das, an old student of Mother Teresa, visits her unexpectedly and says that she wants to join her. She will be the first nun of a religious order yet to exist.

*July 10, 1950: The Order of Missionaries of Charity is authorized by Rome.* Other young women follow Subashini Das at a promising rate. Mother Teresa says, "After 1949, I saw young women arriving one after another. All of them had been students of mine. They wanted to give everything to God and they were in a hurry to do so." On October 7, 1950, the feast of Our Lady of the Rosary, Rome authorizes the Order of the Missionaries of Charity.

Ten women begin their novitiate, which lasts two years.

*August 22, 1952: The home for dying destitutes is opened.* There are nearly thirty women in the order. A dozen of them have made their final vows. There are twelve novices and the rest are postulants. The sisters are still in need of a convent of their own. They are "guests" in a rented flat, donated to them by Michael Gomes. They dedicate themselves to studies and religious formation, while caring for abandoned slum children and sick and dying destitutes.

Mother Teresa manages to acquire a home for the destitutes in Kalighat, a Hindu temple in the heart of Calcutta. The home is opened on August 22, 1952, the feast of Mary Immaculate, and is immediately filled to capacity, which will always be the case through the years in spite of the constant "discharges" (there are always new admittances). The home is named Nirmal Hriday, "Home of the Pure Heart," a name that is just as acceptable to Hindus, who are the great majority of those coming to the home.

*1953: The motherhouse of the Missionaries of Charity is founded.*

After "storming" Heaven with constant prayers, the Missionaries of Charity are able to buy a home for their convent, located at 54 Lower Circular Road in Calcutta. The home is well located for their needs and temporarily spacious. The motherhouse will become the central headquarters for the Missionaries of Charity.

On the same street, the sisters rent and later buy a home for abandoned and orphaned slum children. Many of the parents of these children have died in the home for dying destitutes.

The sisters initially want to open a home as well for the lepers that they care for. However, due to the opposition of the general population, they start up "mobile clinics" for the lepers. Later the sisters will be able to open self-sufficient rehabilitation centers for lepers, called Titagahr and Shanti Nagar, on the outskirts of Calcutta.

*1962: Mother Teresa is honored in Asia.* Mother Teresa is honored with the Padna Sri (Order of the Lotus) Award given to her by the Indian government and the Magsaysay Award given to her by the SEATO nations of southeastern Asia. She is declared the most worthy woman in Asia. However, in the West, she is still largely unknown.

*February 1, 1965: The Missionaries of Charity receive further recognition.* The Missionaries of Charity have now existed for fifteen years. They have had extraordinary growth and expansion. There are approximately three hundred sisters in the order, including sisters of different European nationalities, and several homes. All of the Missionary of Charity homes are still located in India under the jurisdiction of the local Catholic bishops. With the support of several bishops, Pope Paul VI decrees the praiseworthiness of the Missionaries of Charity, giving "validity" to the order for the wider Catholic church. This decree, along with an invitation from the Archbishop of Barquisimeto, Venezuela, to open a home in his diocese, enables the Missionaries of Charity to expand their missionary work.

*1965-71: New homes are opened around the world.* The home in Venezuela is Mother Teresa's first home "abroad." During the following years more homes are opened in Africa, in Australia (Melbourne and Adelaide), and in Europe (England and Italy) as a response to invitations extended by local Catholic bishops. The Missionaries of Charity's first home in Rome, Italy, was founded in response to an invitation extended by Pope Paul VI, as Bishop of Rome. The pope is an admirer and benefactor of Mother Teresa's work. By 1971 the Missionaries of Charity have fifty homes.

*March 26, 1969: The Co-workers of the Missionaries of Charity are officially established.* Mother Teresa's Co-workers, an international organization of lay men and women, become a spiritual reality and an important element for furthering the work of the Missionaries of Charity. It is difficult, if not impossible, to ascertain their number due to their constant growth, as well as a certain carelessness of the Missionaries of Charity in keeping accurate statistics. There have been Co-workers ever since the Missionaries of Charity were first founded. On March 3, 1969, Pope Paul VI approves the statutes for the Co-workers and thereby they become officially affiliated with the Missionaries of Charity.

*July 12, 1972: Mother Teresa's mother, Drana Bernai, dies in Albania.* Her mother wanted to leave Albania in order to see her daughter as well as her son, who lives in Sicily, before she died. The Albanian government refused to grant her permission to leave.

*1974: Mother Teresa's only sister, Aga Bojaxhiu, dies.* Mother Teresa's sister dies in Albania without having the opportunity to see either her sister or brother.

*1970s: Mother Teresa receives major international awards.* During the 1970s, the pen and microphone of Malcolm Muggeridge, a British journalist, make Mother Teresa famous in the West, not only in Catholic circles but in wider society. As a consequence, she is awarded the Good Samaritan Award in the United States, the Templeton Award for Progress in Religion in England, and the Pope John XXIII Peace Prize at the Vatican. On October 17, 1979, Mother Teresa is awarded the most famous international award: the Nobel Peace Prize. Nevertheless, her habitual simplicity and humility are not altered.

*December 10, 1979: Mother Teresa accepts the Nobel Peace Prize.* Mother Teresa accepts her award from the hands of King Olaf V of Norway, in the name of the poor whom she represents and to whom she has dedicated her life.

*1980-85: The Missionaries of Charity open many new homes and are blessed with many new vocations.* In 1980 there are fourteen homes outside of India in places as diverse as Lebanon, West Germany, Yugoslavia, Mexico, Brazil, Peru, Kenya, Haiti, Spain, Ethiopia, Belgium, New Guinea, and Argentina. After the Nobel Peace Prize is awarded, the Missionaries of Charity's rate of expansion is surprising: eighteen new homes are opened in 1981, twelve in 1982, and fourteen in 1983. The Missionaries of Charity are also blessed with an increasing rate of new vocations, making the order an exception in an era of general decline in the number of new vocations for religious orders.

*1986-89: The order enters countries previously closed to missionaries.* The Missionaries of Charity are allowed to open homes in Ethiopia and Southern Yemen. Also they are allowed to come to Nicaragua, Cuba, and Russia, where atheism is actively promoted by the state. In the case of the Soviet Union, one of the fruits of Mikhail Gorbachev's "perestroika" is permission for Mother Teresa to open a home in Moscow.

*February 1986: Pope John Paul II comes to Calcutta.* The pope visits Mother Teresa and sees firsthand the work of the Missionaries of Charity.

*May 21, 1988: The Missionaries of Charity open a shelter in the Vatican.* The Missionaries of Charity open a shelter for the homeless in Rome at the Vatican. It is called "A Gift from Mary" to commemorate the Marian Year. The shelter has seventy-two beds for men and women and two dining halls, one for residents and one for those who stop in. The shelter also has a lounge, an infirmary, and a patio which faces the Pope Paul VI audience hall.

1988-89: *Mother Teresa is hospitalized twice due to heart trouble.* It is not the first time that she has overextended herself to the point of physical exhaustion and been hospitalized. Even the pope asks her to take better care of her health. Her doctors install a pacemaker and order her to take six months of rest.

*April 16, 1990: Mother Teresa steps down as the Superior General of the Missionaries of Charity.* Citing ill health as the main reason, Mother Teresa steps down as the Superior General of her order. Relieved of her responsibilities, she is able to spend more time traveling and visiting various houses of sisters.

*September 1990: Mother Teresa is called out of retirement and re-elected the Superior General of the Missionaries of Charity.*

Recognizing her unique spiritual genius and leadership of the order, the Sisters of the Missionaries of Charity re-elect Mother Teresa as Superior General, even though she is now eighty years old and in ill health.

*January 1991: Mother Teresa appeals to two heads of state to avert the Gulf War.* Presidents George Bush and Saddam Hussein received her impassioned plea on behalf of "the innocent ones" only a short time before war erupted. Two teams of sisters go to Baghdad to minister to those ravaged by war.

*1991-1993: Mother Teresa's health declines.* Her failing heart causes Mother Teresa to collapse first in Tijuana, Mexico and again in Delhi, India. Despite her own suffering, she rallies when she is invited to return to Beijing in October 1993.

*August 30, 1993: Co-Workers disbanded.* The Co-Workers had shared in the work of the Missionaries of Charity for twenty-five years. Her failing health prompted Mother Teresa to instruct that only those who worked directly with the Missionaries of Charity would continue to be called Co-Workers. All others would no longer be formally tied to the Missionaries of Charity.

*February 3, 1994: National Prayer Breakfast, Washington D.C.* Flanked by President and Mrs. Clinton and Vice President and Mrs.

Gore, Mother Teresa spoke as thousands of people listened with rapt attention to her message affirming life and calling for peace. Later, the President thanked her for "her life of commitment," a commitment, he said, that she had "truly lived."

THREE

# *Her Work: A Conversation*

In this interview Mother Teresa talks candidly about the order she founded, about her worldwide work with "the poorest of the poor," and about her faith. It is based on several conversations between Mother Teresa and José Luis Gonzalez-Balado that took place in Spain between 1976 and 1980.

**Q:** *Mother Teresa, do you find it easy to carry out your work among the poor?*

**MT:** Of course it would not be easy without an intense life of prayer and a spirit of sacrifice. It wouldn't be easy either if we didn't see in the poor, Christ, who continues to suffer the sorrows of his passion. At times, we would be happy if we could get the poor to live peacefully with each other. It is so hard for those who have been deprived of their basic needs to live in harmony and support their neighbors, and not see them as dangerous competitors, capable of making their state of misery even worse! That's why we cannot offer them anything but our testimony of love, seeing Christ himself in each one of them, no matter how repugnant they seem to us.

**Q:** *How do you get so many vocations?*

**MT:** God is the one who sends them. They come and see. Sometimes they come from very far away. Many of them first hear about us by what they read in the newspapers.

**Q:** *With the sisters you have available, do you accomplish all that you would like?*

**MT:** Unfortunately, the needs are always greater than our ability to meet them.

**Q:** *Mother Teresa, what moves you to continually open new homes?*

**MT:** If God continues sending us so many vocations without fail, we believe that this is not so we can keep them hidden in convents. Rather God wants to multiply the work of helping the poorest of the poor.

**Q:** *What criteria do you use for opening homes in India and abroad?*

**MT:** We never open any home without already having been invited by the local bishop. In fact, the present requests for help far surpass our capability to meet them. As a general rule based on our constitution, when we receive an invitation to open a new home, we first go and investigate the living conditions of the poor in that area. We never decide to open a home for any other reason than that of serving the poor. Normally, the decision to start a new home follows these investigations, except in cases of the most extreme need.

**Q:** *What importance do you give to outward appearances?*

**MT:** Very little or none. As for our habit, even though the sari is part of our usual way of dressing, we would be willing to modify or relinquish it if we found out that we were not accepted for being dressed that way. We would adopt another form of dress if it were better accepted by the poor wherever we felt called to carry out our work.

**Q:** *What gives you strength to carry out your work?*

**MT:** We are taught from the very first moment to discover Christ under the distressing disguise of the poor, the sick, the outcasts.

Christ presents himself to us under every disguise: the dying, the paralytic, the leper, the invalid, the orphan. It is faith that makes our work, which demands both special preparation and a special calling, easy or at least more bearable. Without faith, our work could become an obstacle for our religious life since we come across blasphemy, wickedness, and atheism at every turn.

**Q:** *In your work, how much importance do you give to religious matters?*

**MT:** We are not simply social workers, but missionaries. Nevertheless, we try to do evangelization exclusively through our work, allowing God to manifest himself in it. We teach catechism to the children in our orphanages. We only take the initiative with adults when they ask for instruction or when they ask us questions about religious matters. All of the sisters receive a good religious formation during their novitiate and more training in later years. We do not like to take the place of others who are more competent in some subjects than we are. For example, we refer more difficult questions to priests, besides those that are obviously related to their ministry. As for the criteria we use to determine our assistance, we never base our assistance on the religious beliefs of the needy but on the need itself. We are not concerned with the religious beliefs of those we help. We only focus on how urgent the need is.

**Q:** *Do the Missionaries of Charity have any preferences among the people they assist?*

**MT:** If there is any, it is for the poorest of the poor, the most abandoned, those who have no one to care for them, the orphans, the dying, the lepers.

**Q:** *According to some, the work of the Missionaries of Charity in the home for the dying destitutes only prolongs the misery of those cared for. Those who are restored to health return to the streets where they will encounter the same problems of disease and misery. What is your response to this?*

**MT:** Whenever it is possible we try not to limit our care to just medical attention. We try to achieve the human and social rehabilitation of those who are restored to health. It is true that in many cases those who recuperate prefer the freedom of the streets to the closed spaces of our surroundings, but this is something that we cannot prevent. We act under the conviction that every time we feed the poor, we are offering food to Christ himself. Whenever we clothe a naked human being, we are clothing Christ himself. Whenever we offer shelter to the dying, we are sheltering Christ himself.

**Q:** *There are those who assert that the medical training of the Missionaries of Charity is too rudimentary for people who care for the seriously ill.*

**MT:** I know that. Our medical training is limited, but we try to offer assistance and care to those who, in most cases, have no one to give them even the most basic medical care.

**Q:** *It has also been said that the care that you give to such desperate cases could be better channeled to those who have a better chance of survival.*

**MT:** We try to help all those who need care, but we give preference to those who have the greatest need of help. We do not turn our backs on anyone. No one is left out of our will to serve. In each suffering brother we see the likeness of Christ suffering in him. Even if we have to narrow our care down to a few, because of necessity or limited resources, our desire is to expand our charity.

**Q:** *At times, there isn't much you do or can do for the dying, is there?*

**MT:** We can, at least, leave them with the impression of something important: that there are people willing to truly love them, because the dying are also children of God, and deserve to be loved as much or maybe even more than anyone else.

**Q:** *Don't you ever experience repugnance in the face of so much misery?*

**MT:** Yes, we carry out our work mainly among the dying, the destitute elderly, poor orphaned children, and lepers. We cannot deny that our work is hard for us in many cases. We don't always carry it out under acceptable conditions. But all of us are better off working among the poor than among the rich. This is our lifetime work. During the novitiate, which lasts two years, we dedicate half the day to carrying out our work among the poor. The novices work under the supervision of older sisters. Then, before making our final vows, we spend several more years serving the poor. Our work becomes almost a habit for us, which makes it easier, instinctive, and natural, without being mechanical.

**Q:** *What significance do you attribute to your mission of assistance?*

**MT:** Our service is not limited to offering just material relief. We want to offer whatever is necessary so that the poorest of the poor don't feel abandoned, and so they realize that there are people who care about them. We want our work to accomplish what a high-level official in our country once said to the sisters: "It is Christ who is again walking among us doing good in favor of men."

**Q:** *What do you do for lepers?*

**MT:** We offer assistance to more than twenty thousand afflicted with this disease just in Calcutta alone, and to fifty thousand in all of India. We realize this is nothing in a country where there are four million victims of leprosy. The first thing we do for those who receive our help is to convince them that they really have this disease. We get the necessary medicines for them and we try to cure them. Today it is not necessary for lepers to live in isolation. If we can help them in time, they can be fully cured. So what the sisters try to do first of all is to convince the people to confront this disease. In India, leprosy is considered a punishment from God. It is part of the religion of the people. The sisters try to do everything possible to cure them and rid them of this belief.

**Q:** *How much do the medicines for each leper cost?*

**MT:** Really, we don't pay for the medicines. They are given to us. We receive medicines from many places, starting with the United States, Germany, France, England, and Switzerland. In any case, they don't cost a lot. I don't have an exact idea of how much each patient's medicine costs.

**Q:** *Do you receive enough to help the lepers?*

**MT:** Yes, for the moment at least, as far as medicines are concerned. We also have to buy vitamin pills, analgesics, and some other health aids. Besides these things, of course, we need other aids like clothing, bandages, basic commodities, antiseptics, deodorizers, and lotions.

**Q:** *From whom do you especially receive aid?*

**MT:** From everyone, thanks be to God. We have Hindu, Muslim, Parsee, Jewish, Buddhist, Protestant, and, naturally, Catholic co-workers and benefactors.

**Q:** *Has it ever occurred to you that you could end up without resources for your works?*

**MT:** We never have any surplus, but we have never lacked what we need. Sometimes it happens in strange ways, almost miraculously. We wake up without resources, with the anguish of not being able to tend to our needy. A few hours later, we almost always see the most unexpected provisions arrive from anonymous donors. From Catholics, Protestants, Buddhists, Jews, Parsees, Muslims, and Hindus. From adherents of any religion or of no religion. From the rich and from the poor.

**Q:** *What is the work you accomplish like?*

**MT:** It is not important work in and of itself, but the humblest that exists. We think that its value comes from the spirit of love for God that inspires it. It is impossible to love God without loving our neighbor. At the same time, no Missionary of Charity forgets the words of Christ: "I was hungry and you gave me to eat" (see Matthew 25:35). This is what we are trying to do: feed, clothe, and visit Christ in the sick, the dying, the lepers, and the abandoned children.

**Q:** *Could you talk about your work with abandoned children?*

**MT:** Yes, we started with them and we are still with them, even though they are not our only work. Orphans and abandoned children are unfortunately the kind of children that are never in short supply. Once in the first years of our work, a policeman brought us a group of children that were caught in the act of stealing. They were too young to send to jail with common criminals. I asked them why they had done it. They explained to me that every evening from five to eight o'clock adults gave them lessons on how to commit robberies.

**Q:** *What kind of a future do the children you rescue have?*

**MT:** I don't believe there is a better way of helping India than to prepare a better tomorrow for today's children. We take care of the poorest of those children, the ones that are picked up in the slums. Each one of them needs a monthly allowance of just a few dollars. It is very moving to see children from other countries—French, English, German, Spanish, Swiss, Danish, and Italian children—donate from their savings. We open a savings account for each child we take in. When the child is older and if he is capable, he receives higher education. We see that those children who do not have the aptitude for higher education receive an education in the trades, so that they will be able to make a living for themselves.

**Q:** *You Missionaries of Charity witness terrible injustices. How do you react to them?*

**MT:** The injustices are there for everyone to see. It is up to large organizations to provide or promote the ways of raising the standard of living of the masses that suffer injustice. We find ourselves in daily contact with those who have been rejected by society. Our first goal is to help these people achieve basic human development. We try to restore the sense of dignity that they should have as human beings, as well as children of the same Father. To accomplish this, we don't look first and see if they are dying or if they have a whole life ahead of them.

Q: *Do you receive any aid from the Indian government?*

MT: We do not receive any direct aid, but we have to recognize that the government helps us in a very effective way by the confidence, esteem, and respect they show us. This helps us in many ways, like getting land for the work we carry out and free transportation on the state railways.

Q: *Do you receive any exemptions from the Indian government? Are you allowed to import everything freely?*

MT: No, not everything, just food, medicines, medical equipment, clothing, and anything else that is needed for our work, such as furniture, typewriters, and sewing machines. We still need an import permit. We receive these things as gifts, and they all go to the poor. Nothing is for business transactions. It all goes to those in need, without regard to their race, beliefs, or religion. And there are so many in need! The only thing we have to do is declare to the government that these are free gifts. Since the government sees where everything goes, we are given the necessary permits. They realize that nothing goes into our pockets. Everything is given back to the poorest of the poor. That's why they trust us and give us the necessary permits.

Q: *How do you manage what you receive?*

MT: We have a register where we write down all our expenses, as well as what we receive and for what purpose we have to earmark these gifts. For example, if someone donates one hundred rupees for the lepers, we don't use that money for anything else. We try to carry out the will of our donors.

Q: *It seems that the Indian government is setting increasingly tighter restrictions on foreign missionaries. Are you affected by this?*

MT: We are a native Indian institution. Our motherhouse is in India. So we don't fall under those restrictions. At the same time, we avoid evangelizing through means other than our work. Our works are our witness. If someone we help wants to become a Catholic, he has to see a priest. If there is a religious end to our work, it is nothing more than to bring all those we have contact with closer to God.

**Q:** *Do you receive any help from others?*

**MT:** Oh, yes! We have counted on the help of others since the very beginning. We call them Co-workers. We have many kinds of Co-workers, starting with the children from many countries who share their savings or the money they collect on drives for the children in India. Even though we Missionaries have the most visibility, really, we could carry out very little of our work without the generous help of thousands upon thousands of Co-workers and friends throughout the world.

**Q:** *Not all religious orders have known how to faithfully keep the initial spirit in which they were founded. Couldn't the Missionaries of Charity lose it also?*

**MT:** Our fourth vow commits us to give free service to the poorest of the poor. This should keep us from the danger you mention. Our mission is so clear that there can be no misunderstandings. The poor know who they are and where they are. They are the reason for our order and our work. In Christ, they are the reason why we exist.

**Q:** *Are you ever tempted with the idea of working among the rich, where everything would be easier for you?*

**MT:** The poor are the reason for our existence. We were born for them and we dedicate ourselves just to them, without any temptation to turn away.

**Q:** *What kind of growth have the Missionaries of Charity experienced?*

**MT:** As I have said, we do not have a crisis in vocations. God is very generous with us and he sends us vocations. Among the young women who ask to join our order, there are those who are college-educated, while others come from the world of work. As for nationalities, the majority are Indian just as our order is. But there are also Irish, Italians, Germans, French, English, Spanish, Portuguese, and Americans. Also we have sisters from Venezuela, Mexico, Peru, and

Brazil. We even have a few from Africa and Australia.

**Q:** *Do you attempt to present any special religious message through your work?*

**MT:** Love has no other message but its own. Every day we try to live out Christ's love in a very tangible way in every one of our deeds. If we do any preaching, it is done with deeds, not with words. That is our witness to the gospel.

**Q:** *You need a lot of money to carry out your mission.*

**MT:** Money is useful, but the love, the attention, and the care we offer to others are the most important things. Love has to begin at home with those around us.

**Q:** *Do you feel loved by the people?*

**MT:** Yes, for the most part, even though the extreme conditions in which many of our people live keeps them from seeing our unconditional love. They see that we live among them and in poverty like they do. They appreciate that a lot. Still, not everything is peaceful all the time. Sometimes there are outbreaks of jealousy or impatience when we can't give them everything they need or ask for, or when they see that we are giving out the very things they want to others more needy than themselves. When that happens, we know it is useless to try to reason with them at that moment. It is best to allow them to calm down. They almost always have a change of attitude once they have calmed down.

**Q:** *Do you witness conversions to Catholicism among the people you help?*

**MT:** Yes, there are some conversions, but without us ever trying to encourage them directly. By practicing Christian love, we draw closer to God and we try to help others draw closer to him, without placing any religious pressure on anyone. When they accept love, they accept God and vice versa. Our witness is none other than that. At the same time it would be a mistake to forget that we find ourselves in India, among a people proud of their cultural and religious traditions. For that very reason they look with distrust upon any form of religious proselytism.

**Q:** *What contact do the Missionaries of Charity have with their families?*

**MT:** Once we are consecrated to serving the poor, they become our family. Naturally we do not deny our blood relationships with our biological families, but contact with them is very limited. Only under extraordinary circumstances, such as before leaving the country for a foreign mission, do we go home. We just cannot do it, first of all because of our poverty; we do not have the money to spend on trips. Second, none of us can leave our post of service and care to the sick, the dying, the lepers, and the orphans when they have no one else to look after them.

**Q:** *What do you think of receiving awards?*

**MT:** The same as always: I don't deserve them. I accept them willingly, not just to acknowledge the kindness of those who give the awards, but I think of what these awards can mean for our poor and our lepers. On the other hand, I think that these awards greatly help people to be favorably inclined toward the work we Missionaries of Charity carry out among the poorest of the poor.

# PART TWO

## *Prayers from the Heart's Fullness*

Mother Teresa is a woman of constant prayer. She prays with her community at Mass every morning before going out to work. She prays again each evening in the quiet chapel. And she prays throughout the day wherever she finds herself.

Part Two includes three of Mother Teresa's favorite prayers: one by a thirteenth-century saint, one by a nineteenth-century theologian, and one taken from words of Scripture. Here also is a prayer from the thirteenth century that beautifully expresses the focus of Mother Teresa's experience with God.

FOUR

# *Make Me An Instrument of Your Peace*

Mother Teresa loves this prayer. She has incorporated it into the daily devotions of her order, the Missionaries of Charity, and she often asks her audiences to say it with her.

The prayer is attributed to St. Francis of Assisi, and it certainly reflects his life.

Francis was born in 1181 or 1182 to a wealthy cloth merchant in central Italy. As a teenager and a young man, he enjoyed parties, mischief, and military skirmishes. But when he was in his mid-twenties, a change began to come over him. More and more, he was attracted to a life of prayer and service to the poor.

On a pilgrimage to Rome, Francis traded clothes with a leper both to help the sick man and to understand how he felt. He sold some of his father's fine cloth to rebuild a ruined church near Assisi. (His father disinherited him for his lack of business sense.) He gathered about him a group of men and women who pledged to live in utter poverty and preach the kingdom of God. Francis's followers quickly began to preach, heal, and pray, not only in Italy but also in Africa, in Asia Minor, and throughout Europe.

St. Francis died in his mid-forties, but his contribution to Christianity still continues eight hundred years later in the Franciscans and the Poor Clares. His devotion to poverty, compassion for the poor, and prayerful contemplation of Christ is a constant source of inspiration to Mother Teresa.

*Lord, make me an instrument of your peace.*
*Where there is hatred, let me sow love;*
*where there is injury, pardon;*
*where there is doubt, faith;*
*where there is despair, hope;*
*where there is darkness, light;*
*where there is sadness, joy.*
*O divine Master, grant that I may not so much seek*
*to be consoled, as to console;*
*to be understood, as to understand;*
*to be loved, as to love.*
*For it is in giving that we receive;*
*it is in pardoning that we are pardoned;*
*it is in dying that we are born to eternal life.*

*Lord, make me an instrument of your peace.*

• Each one of us is merely a small instrument; all of us, after accomplishing our mission, will disappear.

• All of us should work for peace. But to obtain that peace all of us have to learn from Jesus to be meek and humble of heart. Only humility will lead us to unity, and unity to peace. To that end, let us help each other draw closer to Jesus, so that we may learn the lesson of humility with joy.

• We want this year to be, above all, a year of peace. With that aim, we will try to talk more with God than with men.

• Let us spread Christ's peace as he did. He planted good everywhere. He did not forsake his works of charity because the Pharisees and others rejected him and tried to spoil his Father's work. Cardinal Newman wrote: "Make me preach thee without preaching—not by words, but by my example and by the catching force, the sympathetic influence, of what I do—by my visible resemblance to thy saints, and the evident fullness of the love which my heart bears to thee."

• In the world there is too much hatred, too much fighting. We will not be able to put them away with guns or bombs or any kind of weapon that wounds. We will attain that only through gestures of love, of joy, and of peace.

• With the Nobel Peace Prize that I have been given, I will try to build homes for many people who are without shelter. I am convinced that love begins at home. So if we can build more homes for the poor, I think that will make even more love possible among our people. This compassionate love will help us to bring peace, to be the good news to the poor. First, we must bring peace to the poor in our own families. After that, we must bring this peace to the poor in our own country, and from there to the whole world. To be capable of doing this, our sisters' lives must be saturated with prayer. They have to live completely surrendered to Christ, so they can understand and share this peace that God brings. There is so much suffering today.

• Let us give thanks to God for the opportunity that he has given us in our day. Let us thank him for this peace prize which reminds us that we have been created to live in peace. Jesus became man to bring that good news to the poor. Being God, he became like us in every way except sin. And he proclaimed clearly that he had come to bring good news. That good news was God's peace to all men of good will. That peace is something which is fundamental to the satisfaction of our most basic desires. It is a peace of the heart.

• Our works of love are nothing but works of peace. Let us do them with greater love and efficiency. It is always the same Christ who says:

I was hungry—not only for food, but for peace that comes from a pure heart.

I was thirsty—not for water, but for peace that satiates the passionate thirst of passion for war.

I was naked—not for clothes, but for the beautiful dignity of men and women for their bodies.

I was homeless—not for a shelter made of bricks, but for a heart that understands, that covers, that loves.

• In our work we may often be caught in idle conversations or gossip. Let us be well on our guard, for we may be caught while visiting families. We may talk about the private affairs of this or that one and so forget the real aim of our visit. We come to bring the peace of Christ, and what if we are a cause of trouble? How our Lord will be hurt by such conduct! We must never allow people to speak against priests, religious, or their neighbors.

• If we find that a family is in a bad mood and is sure to start a tale of uncharitableness, let us say a fervent prayer for them and then say a few things which may help them to think a little about God; then let us leave the place at once. We can do no good until their restless nerves are at peace. We must follow the same conduct with those who want to talk with the aim of wasting our precious time.

• If each one of us would simply remember that God loves us and is giving us the chance to love others in that love—not so much in big things but in the little things of life—our countries could become full of God's love. And how beautiful it would be if the power of peace would go forth and destroy the power to make war and take life. How great it would be to see the joy of life break forth into the lives of the unborn! If you become this kind of torch lit for peace in the world, then indeed the Nobel Peace Prize will be a true gift from the Norwegian people. God bless you!

*Where there is hatred, let me sow love...*

• "My new commandment: Love one another as I have loved you" (see John 15:12).

"If a man loves me, he will keep my Word.... My Father will love him and we will come to him and make our home with him" (see John 14:21-23).

In loving one another through our works we bring an increase of grace and a growth in divine love. Since Jesus' love is our mutual love, we will be able to love as he loves, and he will manifest himself through us to each other and to the world; by this mutual love they will know that we are his.

• Such is the chain that unites and binds us, the old with the young, a chain of gold, a thousand times stronger than flesh and blood, interest or friendship, because these permit the defects of the body and the vices of the soul to be seen, while charity covers all, hides all, to offer exclusively to admiration and love the work of the hands of God, the price of the blood of Jesus Christ, and the masterpiece of the Holy Spirit.

• Today God loves the world through you and through me. Are we that love and that compassion? God proves that Christ loves us—that he has come to be his Father's compassion. Today God is loving the world through you and through me and through all those who are his love and compassion in the world.

• Jesus came into this world for one purpose. He came to give us the good news that God loves us, that God is love, that he loves you, and he loves me. He wants us to love one another as he loves each one of us. Let us love him. How did the Father love him? He gave him to us. How did Jesus love you and me?—by giving his life. He gave all that he had—his life—for you and me. He died on the cross because he loved us, and he wants us to love one another as he loves each one of us. When we look at the cross, we know how he loved us. When we look at the manger we know how he loves us now, you and me, your family, and everybody's family with a tender love. And God loves us with a tender love. That is all that Jesus came to teach us, the tender love of God. "I have called you by your name, you are mine" (see Isaiah 43:1).

• Charity is patient; it is kind; it is not jealous; it is not malicious, arrogant, or insolent. It is not self-seeking and never aims at evil. It is not pleased with the suffering of others; it rejoices in the victories of good; it has faith and hope and stands until the end (see 1 Corinthians 13:4-7). A Missionary of Charity must be full of charity toward her own soul and must spread this charity among both Christians and pagans.

• We do not need to carry out grand things in order to show a great love for God and for our neighbor. It is the intensity of love we put into our gestures that makes them into something beautiful for God.

• I want you to go and find the poor in your homes. Above all, your love has to start there. I want you to be the good news to those around you. I want you to be concerned about your next-door neighbor. Do you know who your neighbor is? Who are your neighbors?

• Now, more than ever we need to live out the teaching of Jesus: "Love one another, as the Father has loved me." We have to love as the Father loves his Son Jesus, with the same mercy and compassion, joy and peace. Try to find out how the Father loves his Son, and then try to love one another in the same way. Find out in all humility how much you are loved by Jesus. From the time you realize that you are loved by Jesus, love as he loves you.

• Our love for one another will be—
  — selfless, generous, tender, personal, and respectful;
  — beyond likes and dislikes, friendship and enmity, worthiness or unworthiness;
  — faithful, deep, and freeing;
  — not compromising because we care; compassionate and forgiving because we understand;
  — always inspiring, encouraging, trusting, wholehearted, and sacrificial unto the death of the cross.

• "Thou shalt love the Lord thy God with thy whole heart, with thy whole soul, and with all thy mind" (see Deuteronomy 6:5, KJV).

This is the command of our great God, and he cannot command the impossible. Love is a fruit, in season at all times and within the reach of every hand. Anyone may gather it and no limit is set. Everyone can reach this love through meditation, the spirit of prayer, and sacrifices, by an intense interior life. Do I really live this life?

• We must not be ashamed to love Christ with our emotions. A woman loves her husband with her whole heart. In her autobiography, the Little Flower tells about a relative who came to see her. This woman was always talking about her husband, about his long hair, his beautiful eyes, and so on. She expressed her love for him so beautifully. The Little Flower listened to her and then wrote these words in her diary: "I will never allow a woman to love her husband more than I love you, O Jesus Christ."

Jesus was everything to her. She was so attached to Christ. Is it the same for you? Do you love Christ like that? We must love Christ with our emotions. Let us all make use of our ability to love.

Be one with him, joined to him and united to him so that nothing, absolutely nothing, can separate you from the love of Christ. He belongs to you and you belong to him. It's as simple as that. Accept whatever he gives and give whatever he takes with a big smile.

Yet we forget. We can love the leper, the one with the broken and disfigured face, but we forget to love our sister when she is proud or impatient. We forget that it is only a distressing disguise, that the person is really Jesus. We do not have undivided love for Christ but, instead, we let the devil trick us with the distressing disguise. We must be holy. We must be able to see Jesus in our sisters and in the poor.

When the Little Flower was canonized, no great things were uncovered for her canonization. She was canonized for one thing only. As Pius X said, "She did ordinary things with extraordinary love"—small things with great love. This is what you and I gave when we gave our word to Jesus. This is our vow.

• Our holy faith is nothing but a gospel of love, revealing to us God's love for men and claiming in return man's love for God.

"God is love": a missionary must be a missionary of love. We must spread God's love on earth if we want to make souls repent wholeheartedly for sin, to strengthen them in temptation, and to increase their generosity and their desire to suffer for Christ. Let us act Christ's love among men, remembering the words of the *Imitation,* "Love feels no burden, values no labors, would willingly do more than it can, complains not of impossibilities, because it conceives that it may and can do all things; when weary is not tired; when strained is not constrained; when frightened is not disturbed; but like a living flame and torch all on fire, it mounts upwards and securely passes through all opposition."

• In the Scripture we read of the tenderness of God for the world, and we read that God loved the world so much that he gave his Son Jesus to come to be like us and to bring us the good news that God is love, that God loves you and loves me. God wants us to love each other as he loves each one of us. We all know, when we look at the cross, how Jesus loved us. When we look at the Eucharist we know how he loves us now. That's why he made himself the Bread of Life to satisfy our hunger for his love, and then, as if this was not enough for him, he made himself the hungry one, the naked one, the homeless one, so that you and I can satisfy his hunger for our human love. For we have been created for that. We have been created to love and to be loved.

• One day I was walking down the street in London. And I saw a tall, thin man on the corner, all huddled up looking most miserable.

I went up to him, shook his hand, and asked him how he was. Then he looked up at me and said, "Oh! After such a long, long, long time I feel the warmth of a human hand!" And he sat up.

There was such a beautiful smile on his face, because somebody was kind to him. Just shaking his hand had made him feel like somebody.

For me, he was Jesus in a distressing disguise. I gave him the joy of being loved, the feeling of being loved by somebody.

Somebody loves us, too—God himself.

*... where there is injury, pardon...*

• These are the few ways we can practice humility:
To speak as little as possible of oneself.
To mind one's own business.
Not to want to manage other people's affairs.
To avoid curiosity.
To accept contradiction and correction cheerfully.
To pass over the mistakes of others.
To accept insults and injuries.
To accept being slighted, forgotten, and disliked.
Not to seek to be specially loved and admired.
To be kind and gentle even under provocation.
Never to stand on one's dignity.
To yield in discussion even though one is right.
To choose always the hardest.

• In these times of development, the whole world runs and is hurried. But there are some who fall down on the way and have no strength to go ahead. These are the ones we should care about.

• Let us be very sincere in our dealings with each other and have the courage to accept each other as we are. Do not be surprised or become preoccupied at each other's failure; rather see and find the good in each other, for each one of us is created in the image of God. Jesus has said it so beautifully: "I am the vine, you are the branches." Let us try to see and accept that every sister is a branch in Christ the vine. The life-giving sap that flows from the vine through each of the branches is the same.

• If sometimes we feel as if the Master is away, is it not because we have kept ourselves far from someone? One thing will always secure heaven for us: acts of charity and kindness with which we have filled our lives. We will never know how much good just a simple smile can do. We tell people how kind, forgiving, and understanding God is—

are we the living proof? Can they really see this kindness, this forgiveness, this understanding, alive in us?

• Be kind in your actions. Do not think that you are the only one who can do the efficient work, work worth showing. This makes you harsh in your judgment of others who may not have the same talents. God will ask of that sister only what he has given her, and not what he has given you; so why interfere with the plan of God? All things are his, and he gives as he pleases. You do your best and think that others do their best for God's own purpose. Their best may be a total failure—what is that to you? You follow the way he has chosen for you. For others also, let him choose.

• Let us admire Christ's compassion toward Judas. The Master kept a holy silence: he did not want to reveal his betrayer in front of his comrades. Jesus could have easily spoken out and unveiled the hidden intentions of Judas. He preferred mercy rather than condemnation. He called him friend. If Judas had looked in Jesus' eyes, he would surely have been the friend of God's mercy.

*... where there is doubt, faith...*

• Dom Marmion wrote: "All you have to do is abandon yourselves in his hands like wax, so that he will cut without fear the useless parts." For his part, when Dom Marmion underwent the temptation to abandon his order, he prostrated himself in front of the tabernacle and shouted out, "May I be broken into pieces rather than abandon the monastery!"

Are we strong enough, to the point of preferring to be cut into pieces rather than abandon Christ? One cannot change one's profession as easily as one can change dress.

In our day all things grow weaker. Even the most sacred ties are untied. Let us submit to the Rock, who is Christ.

• Be faithful in small things because it is in them that your strength lies. Nothing is small for our good God, for he is great and we are small. That is why he lowers himself and cares to do small things, in order to offer us an opportunity to show him our love. Since he does them, they are great things, they are infinite. Nothing he does can be small.

• Faithfulness to the Rule is the most delicate and precious flower we can offer God. The Rule expresses God's will: we have to submit to it to our last breath.

When the Rule becomes one of the things we love most, that love becomes a free service that is carried out with a smile. Submission, for a person who loves, is more than a duty; it is the secret of holiness.

We are to be persuaded that even the smallest unjustified transgression wounds the heart of Jesus and stains our conscience. We must be faithful in small things, not for themselves—for that would be for petty spirits—but because of God's will, which we always have to respect in small things. The smallest Rule contains God's will, no less than the great things of life.

In order to understand this truth, we must be convinced that the Rule has a divine origin. We must hold fast to it, as a small child holds fast to his mother.

We must love this truth with our will and with our reason. It does not matter if sometimes it seems hard, austere, and artificial. God has been so wonderful to us; it is our duty to be wonderful toward him.

• Faith is a gift from God. Without faith, no life is possible. For our work to bear fruit, for it to belong to God alone, it must be founded on faith. Christ has said, "I was hungry, naked, sick, homeless.... You did it for me" (see Matthew 25:35-40). Our work is founded on faith in these words of Christ. Faith is scarce nowadays because selfishness is quite abundant; personal advantage is sought above all. Faith cannot be genuine without being generous. Love and faith go together; they complement each other.

• **Q:** ***In the event that you had to work in a country where you were only allowed to work for the poor under the condition that you renounce your*** *faith and your religion, would you be capable of staying to help the poor? Or would you have to go elsewhere so you could practice your religion?*

MT: No one can take my religion away from me. They can't prevent me from believing or snatch it away from me. It is something that is inside of me. And if there were no other alternative, if that were the only way that Christ chose to come to those people, then I would stay to serve them. But I would not renounce my faith. I would be willing to lose my life but not my faith.

• [Practice] fidelity in the least things, not for their own sake—for this is the work of small minds—but for the sake of the great thing, which is the will of God and which I respect greatly in little things. St. Augustine says: "Little things are indeed little, but to be faithful in little things is a great thing." Is not our Lord equally present in a small host as in a great one? The smallest rule contains the will of God as much as the big things of life.

• In order for us to be able to love, we need to have faith, because faith is love in action, and love in action is service. This is why Jesus became the Bread of Life: so that we may be able to eat and live and to see him in the faces of the poor. In order for us to be able to love we have to see and touch. And so Jesus made the poor the hope of salvation for you and for me. In fact, Jesus said, "As often as you did it for one of my least brothers, you did it for me" (Mt 25:40).

*... where there is despair, hope...*

• The poor are a hope. They represent, in fact, the hope of the world through their courage. They offer us a different way of loving God, by urging us to do all we can to help them.

*... where there is darkness, light...*

• In the poor neighborhoods we are God's light and kindness.

• Knowledge of Christ and him in his poor will lead us to personal love. This love only can become our light and joy in cheerful service of each other. Do not forget we need each other. Our lives would be empty without each other. How can we love God and his poor if we do not love each other with whom we live and break the Bread of Life daily?

• These words of Jesus, "Love one another, even as I have loved you," should be not only a light to us, but they should also be a flame consuming the selfishness which prevents our growth in holiness. Jesus loved us to the end, to the very limit of love, to the cross. This love must come from within—from our union with Christ. It must be an outpouring of our love for God. Loving must be as normal to us as living and breathing, day after day until our death. To understand this and practice it we need much prayer, the kind that unites us with God and overflows continually upon others. Our works of charity are nothing but the overflow of our love of God from within. Therefore, the one who is most united to him loves her neighbor most.

• Jesus wants us to give of ourselves every moment. You have been taught by those who have given their whole lives to Christ. By their teaching and personal example, they have kindled the light of Christ in your lives. The time has come for you likewise to kindle the same light of Christ in the lives of those around you.

• Listen to what Jesus says: "I want you to be my fire of love among the poor, the dying, and the small. I want you to bring the poor to me." Learn this expression by heart, and repeat it when you lack generosity. We risk rejecting Jesus every time we reject others.

If our attitude is "I will not give you my hands to work, my eyes to see, my legs to walk, my spirit to study, my heart to love. You will knock at my door, but I will not open," then it is a wounded Christ, a battered Christ, a Christ of deformity that we give to others.

If you want others to love him, you must first make him known to them. So give a whole Christ to those who live in the inner city—a Christ full of love, of joy, of light. Do not be a dim light, but a shining light.

• What you contemplatives have to bring is your presence, and by that presence you will bring light. Christ must be the light that shines through you, and the people looking at you must see only Jesus. Don't try to be anything else but that. You have a challenge from Jesus to meet: He has shed the light, and you will take his light and lighten every heart you meet. You will not work in big groups or with big numbers, but in the street, in the hospitals, in the jails: Any place where darkness has surrounded that person, you are to be the light-bearer.

• Do not think that love, in order to be genuine, has to be extraordinary. What we need is to love without getting tired.

How does a lamp burn? Through the continuous input of small drops of oil. If the drops of oil run out, the light of the lamp will cease, and the bridegroom will say, "I do not know you" (see Matthew 25:1-13).

What are these drops of oil in our lamps? They are the small things of daily life: faithfulness, punctuality, small words of kindness, a thought for others, our way of being silent, of looking, of speaking, and of acting. These are the true drops of love that keep our religious life burning like a lively flame.

Do not look for Jesus away from yourselves. He is not out there; he is in you. Keep your lamp burning, and you will recognize him.

• Joy is love, the normal result of a heart burning with love. Our lamp will be burning with sacrifices made out of love if we have joy. Then the Bridegroom will say, "Come and possess the kingdom prepared for you." It is a joyful sister who gives most. Everyone loves the one who gives with joy and so does God. Don't we always turn to someone who will give happily and without grumbling? "Joy is a net of love by which we catch souls." Because we are full of joy, everyone wants to be with us and to receive the light of Christ that we possess.... Daily, we pray, "Help me to spread your fragrance," yours, Lord, not mine.

• My sisters also work in Australia. On the reservation, among the Aborigines, there was an elderly man. I can assure you that you have never seen a situation as difficult as that poor old man's. He was completely ignored by everyone. His home was disordered and dirty.

I told him, "Please, let me clean your house, wash your clothes, and make your bed." He answered, "I'm okay like this. Let it be."

I said again, "You will be still better if you allow me to do it."

He finally agreed. So I was able to clean his house and wash his clothes. I discovered a beautiful lamp, covered with dust. Only God knows how many years had passed since he last lit it.

I said to him, "Don't you light that lamp? Don't you ever use it?"

He answered, "No. No one comes to see me. I have no need to light it. Who would I do it for?"

I asked, "Would you light it every night if the sisters came?"

He replied, "Of course."

From that day on the sisters committed themselves to visiting him every evening. We cleaned the lamp, and the sisters would light it every evening.

Two years passed. I had completely forgotten that man. He sent this message: "Tell my friend that the light she lit in my life continues to shine still."

I thought it was a very small thing. We often neglect small things.

*... where there is sadness, joy.*

• May the joy of the risen Jesus Christ be with you, to bring joy into your very soul. The good God has given himself to us. In return for the great grace of baptism, the priest tells the newly baptized, "May you serve the church joyfully."

• Easter is one of the feasts of our Society, a feast of joy—the joy of the Lord. Let nothing so disturb us, so fill us with sorrow or discouragement, as to make us forfeit the joy of the resurrection.

• May the joy of our risen Lord be your strength in your work, your way to the Father, your light to guide you and your Bread of Life.

• May the joy and love of the risen Jesus be always with you, in you, and among you, so that we all become the true witnesses of his Father's love for the world: "For God loved the world so much that he gave his Son" (see John 3:16). Let us also love God so much that we give ourselves to him in each other and in his poor.

• Joy is not simply a matter of temperament in the service of God and souls; it is always hard—all the more reason why we should try to acquire it and make it grow in our hearts.

• To children and to the poor, to all those who suffer and are lonely, give them always a happy smile; give them not only your care but also your heart. We may not be able to give much but we can always give the joy that springs from a heart that is in love with God. Joy is very infectious. Therefore, be always full of joy when you go among the poor.

• Someone once asked me, "Are you married?" And I said, "Yes, and I find it sometimes very difficult to smile at Jesus because he can be very demanding." This is really something true. And there is where love comes—when it is demanding, and yet we can give it to him with joy.

• Cheerfulness and joy was Our Lady's strength. This made her a willing handmaid of God, her Son, for as soon as he came to her she "went in haste." Only joy could have given her the strength to go in haste over the hills of Judea to do the work of handmaid to her cousin. So with us too; we like her must be true handmaids of the Lord and daily after Holy Communion go in haste, over the hills of difficulties we meet in giving whole-hearted service to the poor. Give Jesus to the poor as the handmaid of the Lord.

• God loves a cheerful giver. He gives most who gives with joy. If in the work you have difficulties and you accept them with joy, with a big smile—in this, as in any other good thing—they will see your good works and glorify the Father. The best way to show your gratitude to God and people is to accept everything with joy. A joyful heart is the normal result of a heart burning with love.

• What is required of a Missionary of Charity is this: health of mind and body; ability to learn; a good dose of good sense; joyous character. If one of my sisters is not in at least a serene mood, I do not allow her to go visit the poor. The poor already have so many reasons to feel sad; how could we take them the affliction of our own personal bad moods?

• Joy is strength. The poor felt attracted to Jesus because a higher power dwelt in him and flowed from him—out of his eyes, his hands, his body—completely released and present to God and to men.

• Strive to be the demonstration of God in the midst of your community. We have to radiate the joy of being poor, with no need for words. We must be happy in our poverty.

• Novices, I desire to hear the music of your smiles of joy.

• People do not seem very willing to see us, but all of them hunger and thirst for what God wants to give them through us. All over the world men are hungry and thirsty for God's love. You meet that hunger by spreading joy.

• In order to spread joy, joy needs to reign in the family. Peace and war start within one's own home. If we really want peace for the world, let us start by loving one another within our families. We will thus have Christ's joy, which is our strength. Sometimes it is hard for us to smile at one another. It is often difficult for the husband to smile at his wife or for the wife to smile at her husband.

• What would our life be like if the sisters were not cheerful? It would be mere slavery. We would work without attracting anybody. Sadness, discouragement, and slowness open the doors for sloth, which is the mother of all evils.

If you are joyful, do not worry about lukewarmness. Joy will shine in your eyes and in your look, in your conversation and in your countenance. You will not be able to hide it because joy overflows. When people see happiness in your eyes, they will become aware of their nature as children of God.

Holy souls sometimes undergo great inward trial, and they know darkness. But if we want others to become aware of the presence of Jesus, we must be the first ones convinced of it.

Imagine a sister who goes to the slums with a sad face and a slow pace. What can her presence convey to poor people? Nothing but a deeper discouragement.

Joy is very contagious. Try, therefore, to be always overflowing with joy whenever you go among the poor.

Joy, according to St. Bonaventure, has been given to man so that he can rejoice in God because of the hope of the eternal good and on the sight of all the benefits he receives from God. Thus he will know how to rejoice at his neighbor's prosperity, how to be pleased in giving glory to God, and how to feel discontent concerning empty things.

• Joy must be one of the pivots of our life. It is the token of a generous personality. Sometimes it is also a mantle that clothes a life of sacrifice and self-giving.

A person who has this gift often reaches high summits. He or she is like a sun in a community. Let those who suffer find in us comforting angels.

Why has the work in the slums been blessed by God? Certainly not because of given personal qualities, but because of the joy that the sisters spread as they pass by.

The people of the world lack our joy. Those who live in the slums have still less of it. Our joy is the best means to preach Christianity to the heathen.

• We should ask ourselves, "Have I really experienced the joy of loving?" True love is love that causes us pain, that hurts, and yet brings us joy. That is why we must pray to God and ask him to give us the courage to love.

• As Jesus' co-workers, one thing we have to learn is to sow joy. We don't need bombs or weapons to bring peace to the world. We need that love and compassion we ask for every day. We need a truly compassionate love—a compassion and love that bring joy and peace. The world is hungry for God.

• To bring joy to us, Jesus became man. Mary was the first one to receive Jesus: "My spirit rejoices in God my Savior" (see Luke 1:47). The child in Elizabeth's womb leapt with joy because Mary carried Jesus to him.

In Bethlehem, joy filled everyone: the shepherds, the angels, the three kings, Joseph, and Mary. Joy was also the characteristic mark of the first Christians. During the persecution, people used to look for those who had this joy radiating on their faces. By that joy, they knew who the Christians were and thus they persecuted them.

St. Paul, whom we are trying to imitate in our zeal, was an apostle of joy. He urged the early Christians to rejoice in the Lord always. Paul's whole life can be summed up in one sentence, "I belong to Christ." Nothing can separate me from the love of Christ, neither suffering nor persecution nor anything (see Romans 8:35-39). "I live, now it is no longer I who live but it is Christ who lives in me" (see Galatians 2:20). That is why St. Paul was so full of joy.

• Joy is a need and a power for us, even physically.

A sister who has cultivated a spirit of joy feels less tired and is always ready to go on doing good.

God is joy. He is love. A sister filled with joy preaches without preaching.

A joyful sister is like the sunshine of God's love, the hope of eternal happiness, the flame of burning love.

In our Society, a cheerful disposition is one of the main virtues required for a Missionary of Charity. The spirit of our Society is total surrender, loving trust, and cheerfulness. That is why the Society expects us to accept humiliations readily and with joy; to live the life of poverty with cheerful trust; to imitate the chastity of Mary, the cause of our joy; to offer cheerful obedience from inward joy; to minister to Christ in his distressing disguise with cheerful devotion.

*O divine Master, grant that I may not so much seek*
*to be consoled, as to console;*
*to be understood, as to understand;*
*to be loved, as to love.*

• The more repugnant the work, the greater should be our faith and cheerful devotion. That we feel repugnance is but natural, but when we overcome it for love of Jesus we may become heroic. Very often it has happened in the lives of the saints that a heroic overcoming of repugnance has been what has lifted them to sanctity. This was the case with St. Francis of Assisi, who, when meeting a completely disfigured leper, drew back. But then, overcoming himself, he kissed the terrible, disfigured face. The result was that Francis was filled with an untold joy. He became the complete master of himself, and the leper walked away praising God for his cure.

• Thoughtfulness is the beginning of great sanctity. If you learn this art of being thoughtful, you will become more and more Christlike, for his heart was meek and he always thought of others. Jesus "went about doing good" (see Acts 10:38). Our Lady did nothing else in Cana, but thought of the need of the others and made their need known to Jesus. The thoughtfulness of Jesus and Mary and Joseph was so great that it made Nazareth the abode of God Most High. If we also have that kind of thoughtfulness for each other, our communities will really become the abode of God Most High.

• How beautiful our convents will become where there is this total thoughtfulness of each other's needs! The quickest and the surest way is the tongue: use it for the good of others. If you think well of others, you will also speak well of others and to others. From the abundance of the heart the mouth speaks. If your heart is full of love, you will speak of love.

• How beautiful it is to see the love for each other a living reality! Young sisters, have deep love and respect for your older sisters. Older sisters, treat your younger sisters with respect and love, for they, like you, belong to Jesus. He has chosen each one of you for himself, to be his love and his light in the world. The simplest way of becoming his light is by being kind and loving, thoughtful, and sincere with each other: "By this they will know that you are his disciples" (see John 13:35).

• We have all tried in some way or another to be a real joy to Our Lady. So often during the day, we call her the "cause of our joy" because the joy of her Son is our strength. Let us promise that we will make our community another Bethlehem, another Nazareth. Let us love each other as we love Jesus. In Nazareth there was love, unity, prayer, sacrifice, and hard work; and there was especially a deep understanding and appreciation of each other and thoughtfulness for each other.

• It may happen that a mere smile, a short visit, the lighting of a lamp, writing a letter for a blind man, carrying a bucket of charcoal, offering a pair of sandals, reading the newspaper for someone—something small, very small—may, in fact, be our love of God in action.

•There are many medicines and cures for all kinds of sick people. But unless kind hands are given in service and generous hearts are given in love, I do not think there can ever be any cure for the terrible sickness of feeling unloved.

• The first listening groups have begun to bud among our Co-workers. Those who make up these groups visit the elderly—sometimes in very common and poor houses—and sit down, just letting them talk on and on. The elderly enjoy having someone who listens to them, even when the things they have to say go back to twenty or thirty years ago. Listening, when no one else volunteers to do it, is no doubt a very noble thing.

• My vows bind me to my sister because she is much poorer than the poor outside. If I am not kind and do not smile to the poor outside, someone else will. But for my sister there is no one else.

• Be kind, very kind, to the suffering poor. We little realize what they go through. The most difficult part is the feeling of not being wanted. This is the first hardship a leper experiences, even today. Show your love for them by being very kind—act kindly, speak kindly. I prefer our sisters to make mistakes through kindness than to work miracles through harshness and unkindness.

• Kindness has converted more people than zeal, science, or eloquence. We take a vow to give wholehearted service to the poor. Does this not mean love of the poor? The poor are not at our service. If we want the poor to see Christ in us, we must first see Christ in the poor.

• Holiness grows so fast where there is kindness. I have never heard of kind souls going astray. The world is lost for want of sweetness and kindness. In religious houses this kindness is in greater danger, for we have grown so much used to each other that some think they are free to say anything to anybody at any time. They expect the other sisters to bear with their unkindness. Why not try first to put a brake on your own tongue? You know what you can do, but you do not know how much the other can bear. Why not give the chance of holiness to yourself first? Your holiness will be of greater help to your sisters than the chance you give her to put up with your unkindness.

• The only thing Jesus has asked us to be is meek and humble of heart, and to do this, he has taught us to pray. He has put "meek" first. From that one word comes gentleness, thoughtfulness, simplicity, generosity, truthfulness. For whom? For one another. Jesus put "humility" after meekness. We cannot love one another unless we hear the voice of God in our hearts.

• One year I wanted to do something special for our sisters. I sent out a newsletter to each one of them, to each community, suggesting that each one write down what she thought was beautiful in her sisters and in her community. I asked that each sister send her answer to me. Just imagine! A thousand letters arrived. I had to sit down and patiently read each one, making a list of each community and all the sisters. Later I returned the letters to the communities.

The sisters were surprised that someone would notice such beautiful things in them—that there was someone who was able to see them. All of this fostered a beautiful spirit of love, understanding, and sharing.

I feel that we too often focus only on the negative aspect of life, on what is bad. If we were more willing to see the good and the beautiful things that surround us, we would be able to transform our families. From there, we would change our next-door neighbors and then others who live in our neighborhood or city. We would be able to bring peace and love to our world which hungers so much for these things.

• Let us understand the tenderness of God's love. For he speaks in the Scripture, "Even if a mother could forget her child, I will not forget you. I have carved you on the palm of my hand" (see Isaiah 49:15-16). When you feel lonely, when you feel unwanted, when you feel sick and forgotten, remember you are precious to him. He loves you. And show that love for one another, for this is all that Jesus came to teach us.

• Our Lord, at his dying moment, thought of his mother. That is the proof that he was human to the last. Therefore, if you have a loving nature, keep it and use it for God; if you have a genial temperament that causes you to smile, keep it and use it for God.

*For it is in giving that we receive...*

• May God give back to you in love all the love you have given and all the joy and peace you have sown around you, all over the world. May God bless you deeply.

• Those who helped us during the difficulties that the Bengali refugees underwent claimed that they had received more from those they helped than they had been able to give. This is exactly what each one of us experiences when we come in touch with the poorest poor.

• I am convinced that today's youth are more generous than those of times past. Our youth are better prepared and more willing to sacrifice for the service of man. For that reason, it is no surprise that young people have a preference for our congregation. To a large extent these are young people from the middle class. They have everything: wealth, comfort, high status. However, they ask to enter a congregation that is at the service of the poor, in order to lead a life of real poverty and contemplation.

• Sometimes the rich seem very willing to share in their own way the unhappiness of others. But it is a pity that they never give to the point of feeling that they are in need.

The present generations, especially children, understand better. There are English children who make sacrifices in order to be able to offer a muffin to our children. There are Danish children who make sacrifices in order to be able to offer others a glass of milk every day. And German children do the same in order to be able to offer the poor some fortified food.

These are concrete ways of teaching love. When these children grow up, they will know what it means to give.

• I would like Co-workers to put their hands and their hearts at the service of others. If they do not make contact with the poor, they will not be able to know who they are.

Here in Calcutta we have a number of non-Christians and Christians who work together in the house of the dying and other places. There are also some who offer their care to the lepers.

One day an Australian man came and made a substantial donation. But as he did this he said, "This is something external. Now I want to give something of myself." He now comes regularly to the house of the dying to shave the sick men and to converse with them.

This man gives not only his money but also his time. He could have spent it on himself, but what he wants is to give himself.

• I often ask for gifts that have nothing to do with money. There are things one can get. What I desire is the presence of the donor, for him to touch those to whom he gives, for him to smile at them, for him to pay attention to them. All of this is very meaningful for those people.

• I urge people to join our work for our profit and for the profit of everyone. I never ask them for money or any material thing. I ask them to bring their love, to offer the sacrifice of their hands. When these people run across those in need, their first move is to do something. When they come the second time, they already feel committed. After some time they feel they belong to the poor and that they are filled with the need to love. They discover who they are and what it is that they themselves can give.

• In all our houses and in the novitiate God grants generosity to the religious sisters. Preserve that generosity—you will have all reason to feel happy. Continue smiling at Jesus, through a smile at your superiors, at your sisters, at the poor.

• I think that a person who is attached to riches, who lives with the worry of riches, is actually very poor. If this person puts his money at the service of others, then he is rich, very rich.

• If our poor die of hunger, it is not because God does not care for them. Rather, it is because neither you nor I are generous enough. It is because we are not instruments of love in the hands of God to give them food and clothing. We do not recognize Christ when once again he appears to us under the appearance of suffering—in the hungry man, in the lonely, in the child who is looking for a place where he can get warm.

• I will tell you a story. One night a man came to our house and told me, "There is a family with eight children. They have not eaten for days." I took some food with me and went.

When I came to that family, I saw the faces of those little children disfigured by hunger. There was no sorrow or sadness in their faces, just the deep pain of hunger.

I gave the rice to the mother. She divided the rice in two, and went out, carrying half the rice. When she came back, I asked her, "Where did you go?" She gave me this simple answer, "To my neighbors—they are hungry also!"

Her neighbors were Muslims. I was not surprised that she gave, because poor people are really very generous. But I was surprised that she knew they were hungry. As a rule, when we are suffering, we are so focused on ourselves we have no time for others. This woman showed something of the truly generous love of Christ.

• The other day, two friends of mine came to see me. They brought me a large amount of money to use for feeding the poor. (You must know that just in Calcutta we feed around nine thousand people daily.) I asked them, "Where did you get all that money?"

They answered, "We were married two days ago, but before that we had decided not to have a large wedding banquet. As a witness of our love for each other, we wanted to bring this money to Mother Teresa."

This is the greatness of young people! They are so generous! I asked them further, "Why did you do this?"

They answered, "We love each other so very much, that we wanted to share our love with other people, especially with those you are serving."

• I will never forget how a little four-year-old Hindu child taught me how to show great love. It was a time when we had no sugar in Calcutta. I do not know how that little one heard that Mother Teresa had no sugar for her children. He went home to his parents and told them, "I will not eat sugar for three days. I'll give my sugar to Mother Teresa." That little one loved with great love. He loved until it hurt. And so must we.

• Some time ago I made a trip to Ethiopia. Our sisters were working there during that terrible drought. Just as I was about to leave for Ethiopia, I found myself surrounded by many children.

Each one of them gave something, "Take this to the children! Take this to the children!" they would say. They had many gifts that they wanted to give to our poor.

Then a small child, who for the first time had a piece of chocolate, came up to me and said, "I do not want to eat it. You take it and give it to the children."

This little one gave a great deal, because he gave it all, and he gave something that was very precious to him.

Have you ever experienced the joy of giving? I do not want you to give me from your abundance. I never allow people to have fund-raisers for me. I don't want that. I want you to give of yourself.

The love you put into the giving is the most important thing. If you want a happy family, if you want a holy family, learn to share. Give your hands to serve and your hearts to love.

• For some time now, we have had a small community of sisters in Guatemala. We came there during the earthquake of 1972 which caused so much damage.

The sisters in Guatemala came to love and serve as they do everywhere. They told me something beautiful about a very poor man who was picked up from the city streets and brought to one of our homes. He was very sick, disabled, hungry, helpless. But somehow, with the help of everybody, he got well again.

He told the sisters, "I want to go and leave this bed for somebody else who may need it as much as I needed it when I came here."

And I believe now he has a job. I don't think he earns much, but he is working. Every time he gets a little money, he remembers the other disabled people who are in the home and comes to see them.

He always brings something for them.

Even with the little he has, he always brings something.

This is the great gift of our poor people: the love they have.

• I don't want people donating just to get rid of something. There are people in Calcutta who have so much money that they want to get rid of it. The government puts pressure on the wealthy. They sometimes have money to spare, money that they try to hide. In some cases they make a package, write the name of Mother Teresa on it, and then send it.

A few days ago I received a package wrapped in plain paper. I thought that it might contain stamps, cards, or something like that, so I put it aside. I planned to open it later when I had the time. A few hours later I opened it without even suspecting its contents. It was hard for me to believe my eyes. That package contained twenty thousand rupees. It didn't have a return address or any note, which made me think that it might be money owed to the government.

I don't like people to send me something because they want to get rid of it. Giving is something different. It is sharing.

• Not so long ago a very wealthy Hindu lady came to see me. She sat down and told me, "I would like to share in your work." In India, more and more people like her are offering to help. I said, "That is fine." The poor woman had a weakness that she confessed to me. "I love elegant saris." Indeed, she had on a very expensive sari that probably cost around eight hundred rupees. Mine cost only eight rupees. Hers cost one hundred times more.

Then I asked the Virgin Mary to help me give an adequate answer to her question of how she could share in our work. It occurred to me to say to her, "I would start with the saris. The next time you go buy one, instead of paying eight hundred rupees, buy one that costs five hundred. Then with the extra three hundred rupees, buy saris for the poor."

The good woman now wears 100-rupee saris, and that is because

I have asked her not to buy cheaper ones. She has confessed to me that this has changed her life. She now knows what it means to share. That woman assures me that she has received more than what she has given. That is the way it is with our Co-workers.

• We need to bring prayer into our family life. Through prayer, we will be able to teach our children and relatives to share. We will get more through genuine prayer than with mere words. We should not use words alone to convince people to give us money. Prayer and our words of request must go together. We can't do one without the other. They have to complement each other.

• We need money, medicines, clothing, and a thousand other things for the poor we serve. If so many people weren't generous, thousands would be left unaided. Because we still have many poor, needy children and families that live in the streets—not only in Calcutta but in London, Rotterdam, Madrid, Marseilles, and Rome—the need is great. In the last city I mentioned, we have many needy. The sisters go out at night into the streets, especially around the train station, between 10 P.M. and 2 A.M. to pick up the homeless and take them to the home we have on San Gregorio al Cielo.

The last time that I was in Rome, I found it unbearable to see so many homeless people living that way. So I went to see the mayor of Rome and said, "Give me a place for these people, because they refuse to come with us and would rather stay where they are." He and his staff responded wonderfully. In a few days they offered us a very nice place near the Termini Train Station. At present, all those who have nowhere else to spend the night, except in the streets, go there and sleep in beds. In the morning they leave.

• I don't want you to give me what you have left over. I want you to give from your want until you really feel it!

The other day I received fifteen dollars from a man who has been paralyzed for twenty years. The paralysis only allows him the use of his right hand. The only company he tolerates is tobacco. He told me, "I have stopped smoking for a week. I'm sending you the money I've saved from cigarettes." It must have been a horrible sacrifice for him.

But look at the beauty of his act of sharing. I bought bread with his money, and I gave it to those who were hungry. So both the giver and those who received experienced joy: the paralytic in giving and the poor in receiving.

This is something all of us need to learn. The chance to share our love with others is a gift from God. May it be for us just as it was for Jesus. Let's love one another as he has loved us. Let's love one another with undivided love. Let's experience the joy of loving God and loving one another.

• Do we treat the poor as our dustbins to give whatever we cannot use or eat? I cannot eat this food so I will give it to the poor. I cannot use this thing or that piece of cloth so I will give it to the poor. Am I then sharing the poverty of the poor? Do I identify myself with the poor I serve? Am I one with them? Do I share with them as Jesus shared with me?

This is the wonderful part of our vocation, that as Missionaries of Charity we have created an awareness of the poor in the whole world. Twenty years ago no one would believe that there were hungry, naked men and women around. Today the whole world knows our poor because of our work. Because they know they want to share.

The other day a group of Hindu school children came from very far. They had won prizes in a contest at school and had asked the headmistress to give them money instead of the prizes. Then they said, "Now, take us to Mother Teresa. We want to give this money to her poor people." How wonderful it was that they did not use that money for themselves! Because we have created this awareness the whole world wants to share with the poor.

Whenever I accept money or an award, I always take it in the name of the poor, whom they recognize in me. What am I? I am nothing. It is the poor whom they recognize in me and that they want to give to, because they see what we do. Today people in the world want to see. Why is our congregation spread all over the world today? It is because people see what we do: feeding the hungry Christ, clothing the naked Christ, taking care of the sick, the dying, the leprosy patients. Because they see, they believe. How sad it will be if we are not sincere in what we do.

• We who know Jesus, who love Jesus, who are even consecrated to Jesus, have to love as Jesus has loved. He has given us the Bread of Life so that we may love as he has loved us. He continues to say, "As the Father has loved me, so I have loved you" (Jn 15:9). How has Jesus loved us? By giving himself to us. This is how we are to love each other: by giving ourselves to each other, giving ourselves to the point of feeling pain.

*... it is in pardoning that we are pardoned...*

• We shall always keep in mind that our community is not composed of those who are already saints, but of those who are trying to become saints. Therefore we shall be extremely patient with each other's faults and failures.

• None of us has the right to condemn anyone. Even though we see some people doing something bad, we don't know why they are doing it. Jesus invites us not to pass judgment. Maybe we are the ones who have helped make them what they are. We need to realize that they are our brothers and sisters. That leper, that drunkard, and that sick person is our brother because he too has been created for a greater love. This is something that we should never forget. Jesus Christ identifies himself with them and says, "Whatever you did to the least of my brethren, you did it to me." That leper, that alcoholic, and that beggar is my brother. Perhaps it is because we haven't given them our understanding and love that they find themselves on the streets without love and care.

• It may happen that children repeatedly fail in their religious examination when being prepared for First Communion. Do not give in to discouragement. No more must you do so when you try to settle a marriage or convert a sinner and you do not succeed. If you are discouraged it is a sign of pride because it shows you trust in your own powers. Never bother about people's opinions. Be humble and you will never be disturbed.

• I have experienced many human weaknesses, many human frailties, and I still experience them. But we need to use them. We need to work for Christ with a humble heart, with the humility of Christ. He comes and uses us to be his love and compassion in the world in spite of our weaknesses and frailties.

***... it is in dying that we are born to eternal life.***

• Death is the most decisive moment in human life. It is like our coronation: to die in peace with God. I have never seen anyone die desperate or blaspheming. They all die serenely, almost with joy.

• One day I picked up a man from the gutter. His body was covered with worms.

I brought him to our house, and what did this man say?

He did not curse. He did not blame anyone. He just said, "I've lived like an animal in the street, but I'm going to die like an angel, loved and cared for!"

It took us three hours to clean him. Finally, the man looked up at the sister and said, "Sister, I'm going home to God." And then he died.

I've never seen such a radiant smile on a human face as the one I saw on that man's face. He went home to God.

See what love can do!

It is possible that young sister did not think about it at the moment, but she was touching the body of Christ. Jesus said so when he said, "As often as you did it for one of my least brothers, you did it for me" (Mt 25:40).

And this is where you and I fit into God's plan.

He has kindled his love in our hearts, so that we may love those we meet with his love.

• Very often we pick up sick and dying destitutes from the streets of Calcutta. In twenty-five years we have picked up more than thirty-six thousand people from the streets and more than eighteen thousand have died a most beautiful death. When we pick them up from the street like that, we give them a plate of rice. In no time we revive them. A few nights ago we picked up four people. One was in a most terrible condition, covered with wounds, her body full of maggots. I told the sisters that I would take care of her while they attended to the other three. I really did all that my love could do for her. I put her in bed and then she took hold of my hand. She had such a beautiful smile on her face and she said only: "Thank you." Then she died. There was a greatness of love. She was hungry for love, and she received that love before she died. She spoke only two words, but her understanding love was expressed in those two words. I have never seen a smile like that.

• I am more than sure that all these people who have died with us are in heaven. They are genuine saints. They are already in the presence of God. Perhaps they were not loved on earth, but they are favorite children of God. Therefore I want to pray and to thank God for all the beautiful things that my sisters have done in the house of the dying. Even though that house is a part of the temple of Kali, the goddess of terror, what reigns there above all is the joy of helping the ill to die in peace with God.*

• In New York we have a home for AIDS patients who are dying from what I call "the leprosy of the West." On Christmas Eve, I opened this house as a gift to Jesus for his birthday. We started with fifteen beds for some poor AIDS patients and for four young men I brought out of jail because they didn't want to die there. They were our first guests.

---

* Editor's note. Mother Teresa opened the home for the dying at the Hindu temple for the goddess Kali, or *Kalighat,* on August 22, 1952.

I had made a little chapel for them. There these young people, who had not been near Jesus, or used to praying or confession, could come back to him if they wanted to. Thanks to God's blessing and his love, their hearts completely changed.

Once when I went there, one of them had to go to the hospital. He said to me, "Mother Teresa, you are my friend. I want to speak to you alone." So the sisters went out, and he spoke.

And what did this man say? This was someone who hadn't been to confession or received Holy Communion in twenty-five years. In all those years, he had had nothing to do with Jesus.

He told me, "You know, Mother Teresa, when I get a terrible headache, I compare it with the pain that Jesus had when they crowned him with thorns. When I get that terrible pain in my back, I compare it with Jesus when he was scourged. When I get that terrible pain in my hands and feet, I compare it with the pain Jesus had when they crucified him. I ask you to take me back home. I want to die with you."

I got permission from the doctor to take him back home with me. I took him to the chapel.

I have never seen anybody talk to God the way that young man talked to him. There was such an understanding love between Jesus and him. After three days, he died.

It is hard to understand the change that young man experienced. What brought it about? It was probably the tender love the sisters gave him that made him understand God loved him.

• As Christians, we have been created for great things. We have been created to be holy since we have been created in the image of God. For that reason, when someone dies that person is meant to go home to God. That is where we are all meant to go. Death can be something beautiful. It is like going home. He who dies in God goes home even though we naturally miss the person who has gone. But it is something beautiful. That person has gone home to God.

FIVE

# *Shine Through Me*

Mother Teresa loves this prayer by John Henry Newman, a nineteenth-century English theologian and cardinal. At the end of each day's Mass, the Missionaries of Charity pray it together.

*Dear Lord, help me to spread your fragrance wherever I go. Flood my soul with your spirit and life. Penetrate and possess my whole being so utterly that all my life may only be a radiance of yours.*

*Shine through me, and be so in me that every soul I come in contact with may feel your presence in my soul. Let them look up and see no longer me, but only you, O Lord! Stay with me, then I shall begin to shine as you do; so to shine as to be a light to others. The light, O Lord, will be all from you; none of it will be mine; it will be you shining on others through me. Let me thus praise you in the way you love best, by shining on those around me.*

*Let me preach you without preaching, not by words but by my example, by the catching force, the sympathetic influence of what I do, the evident fullness of the love my heart bears to you. Amen.*

The prayer is based on Jesus' words in the Sermon on the Mount: "You are the light of the world. A city set on a hill cannot be hidden. Men do not light a lamp and then put it under a bushel basket. They set it on a stand where it gives light to all in the house. In the same way, your light must shine before men, so that they may see goodness in your acts and give praise to your heavenly Father" (Mt 5:14-16).

Mother Teresa has given her life to letting Jesus shine through her. She does not preach about Jesus very often. She doesn't need to: people see Jesus in her, because she is doing his work in his spirit.

*Dear Lord, help me to spread your fragrance wherever I go. Flood my soul with your spirit and life. Penetrate and possess my whole being so utterly that all my life may only be a radiance of yours....*

• Jesus has chosen us for himself; we belong to him. Let us be so convinced of this belonging that we do not allow anything, however small, to separate us from this belonging—from this love.

• While we are preparing for the coming of the Holy Spirit, I pray for you that the Holy Spirit may fill you with his purity, so that you can see the face of God in each other and in the faces of the poor you serve. I ask the Holy Spirit to free you of all impurity—body, soul, mind, will, and heart—that each one of you become the living tabernacle of God Most High, and so become a carrier of God's love and compassion. Ask the Holy Spirit to make you a sinner without sin.

• The Scriptures tell us, "I have called you by name. You belong to me. You are precious to me. I love you." God himself declares that we are precious to him. He loves us, and he wants us to respond to his love. In a special way, this refers to those of us who have committed ourselves to belong to God. Your vocation, as well as mine, can be summed up this way: to belong to Jesus, to love with the conviction that nothing and no one can ever separate us from the love of Christ. We want to love him with an undivided love through chastity. We want to embrace poverty willingly for him. We want to surrender ourselves freely. We want to give of ourselves generously through obedience and service to the poor.

• Our ideal is no one but Jesus. We must think as he thinks, love as he loves, wish as he wishes; we must permit him to use us to the full.

It is beautiful to see the humility of Christ—"Who, being in the form of God, thought it not robbery to be equal with God: But made himself, of no reputation, and took upon him the form of a servant, and was made in the likeness of men" (Phil 2:6-7, KJV).

• One day St. Margaret Mary asked Jesus, "Lord, what wilt thou have me to do?" "Give me a free hand," Jesus answered. He will perform the divine work of sanctity, not you, and he asks only for your docility. Let him empty and amend you, and afterwards fill the chalice of your heart to the brim, that you in your turn may give of your abundance. See him in the tabernacle; fix your eyes on him who is the light; bring your hearts close to his divine heart; ask him to grant you the grace of knowing him, the love of loving him, the courage to serve him. Seek him fervently.

• If you give to the people a broken Christ, a lame Christ, a crooked Christ, deformed by you, that is all they will have. If you want them to love him, they must know him first. Therefore, give the whole Christ first to the sisters, then to the people in the slums: Christ full of zeal, love, joy, and sunshine. Do I come up to the mark? Am I a dark light, a false light, a bulb without the connection, having no current, therefore shedding no radiance? Put your heart into being a bright light. Say to Christ, "Help me to shed thy fragrance everywhere I go."

• Let the poor, seeing you, be drawn to Christ. Poverty makes people very bitter, and they speak and act without realizing what they do. But do they remember Christ when they see you—even if they get angry—because you remind them of Christ? Draw them to God but never, never to yourself. If you are not drawing them to God, then you are seeking yourself, and people love you for yourself and not because you remind them of Christ.

• Don't search for Jesus in far lands—he is not there. He is close to you; he is with you. Just keep the lamp burning and you will always see him. Keep on filling the lamp with all these little drops of love, and you will see how sweet is the Lord you love.

• Spiritual life is union with Jesus—the divine and the human in mutual giving. The only thing Jesus asks is that I commit myself to him, in total poverty, in total forgetfulness of self.

• A Missionary of Charity is a messenger of God's love, a living lamp that offers its light to all. We are to take Christ to those places where he has not yet been taken.

The sisters ought to feed only one desire: Jesus. We must not be afraid to do what he has done. We must courageously face danger and death itself for his love and with his help.

A Missionary will always carry Christ's interest in her heart and in her spirit. The fire of love must be lodged in her heart. This love forces her to give herself tirelessly. This becomes her aim and her glory.

*Shine through me, and be so in me that every soul I come in contact with may feel your presence in my soul. Let them look up and see no longer me, but only you, O Lord! Stay with me, then I shall begin to shine as you do; so to shine as to be a light to others. The light, O Lord, will be all from you; none of it will be mine; it will be you shining on others through me. Let me thus praise you in the way you love best, by shining on those around me....*

• We are like machines. When one little thing in the machine is not working, then the whole machine is not working properly.

• The Little Flower, St. Thérèse of Lisieux, said: "When I act and think with charity, I feel it is Jesus who works within me. The closer I am united with him, the more I love all the other dwellers in Carmel." To understand this and practice it we need much prayer, which unites us with God and overflows continually upon others. Our works of charity are nothing but the overflow of our love for

God from within. Therefore the one who is most united to him loves her neighbor most.

• Christ's life was not written while he was living, even though he accomplished the most important work that exists: redeeming the world and teaching mankind to love his Father. Our work is Christ's work, and so we have to be his instruments, to carry out our small task and to disappear.

• We should not be afraid to give Jesus to others. We should not be afraid to put our love into action. We should not be afraid to pray, to work, and to make our work a prayer. This is what a distinguished person in India said: "When I see the sisters in the streets of Calcutta, I always have the impression that Jesus Christ has come again into the world and that he is again going about, doing good works through the sisters." These words, expressed in such a beautiful way, are moving to me. I like to repeat them to everyone, especially to you, my Co-workers. Through your deeds done to help the poor, Christ is going about doing good. Those who see us will see Christ in us.

• As Jesus can no longer live his passion in his body, Mother Church gives the opportunity to allow Jesus to live his passion and death in our body, heart, and soul. Even so, there is no comparison with his passion. Still we need so much grace just to accept whatever he gives and give whatever he takes with joy, love, and a smile.

• You may be writing, and the fullness of your heart will come to your hand also. Your heart may speak through writing. Your heart may speak through your eyes also. You know that when you look at people they must be able to see God in your eyes. If you get distracted and worldly then they will not be able to see God like that. The fullness of our heart is expressed in our eyes, in our touch, in what we write, in what we say, in the way we walk, the way we receive, the way we need. That is the fullness of our heart expressing itself in many different ways.

• I wish to live in this world which is so far from God, which has turned so much from the light of Jesus, to help them—our poor—to take upon me something of their sufferings. For only by being one with them can we redeem them, that is, by bringing God into their lives and bringing them to God.

• The special aim of the Society is to labor at the conversion and sanctification of the poor in the slums; that is, by nursing the sick and the dying, by gathering and teaching little street children, by visiting and caring for beggars and their children, by giving shelter to the abandoned. To labor at the conversion and sanctification of the poor in the slums involves hard, ceaseless toiling, without results, without counting the cost. To convert and sanctify is the work of God, but God has chosen the Missionaries of Charity in his great mercy to help him in his own work. It is a special grace granted to the Missionaries of Charity, without any merit of theirs, to carry the light of Christ into the dark holes of the slums. "I have other food to eat that you know not of. Lift up your eyes and see the fields, white and ready for the harvest" (see John 4:32-35). This is my food, the conversion and sanctification of souls.

• When we do "our work," visiting the families, teaching the children, nursing the sick, helping the dying, gathering the little children for church, we should do it with one aim in view: the salvation of the poor. We want to bring them to Jesus and bring Jesus to them.

The knowledge we impart must be that of Jesus crucified. St. Augustine says: "Before allowing his tongue to speak, the apostle ought to raise his thirsting soul to God, and then give forth what he has drunk in and pour forth what he has been filled with."

Zeal for souls is the effect and the proof of true love of God. If we really love God, we cannot but be consumed with the desire of saving souls, the greatest and the dearest interest of Jesus. Therefore, zeal is the test of love and the test of zeal is devotedness to his cause—spending our life and energy in the work for souls.

• We have to carry our Lord to places where he has not walked before. Therefore the sisters must be consumed with one desire:

Jesus. Speak of no one but him crucified. We must not be afraid to do the things he did—to go fearlessly through death and danger with him and for him.

A "missionary" carries the interest of Christ continually in her heart and mind. In her heart there must be the fire of divine love and of zeal for God's glory and for the salvation of souls. This love makes her spend herself without ceasing. This becomes her real object in life and her joy.

The missionary must die daily, if she wants to bring souls to God. She must be ready to pay the price he paid for souls, to walk in the way he walked.

• Our holy faith is nothing but a gospel of love, revealing to us God's love for men and women and claiming in return their love for God. God is love. A missionary must be a missionary of love. We must spread God's love on earth if we want to make souls repent wholeheartedly for sin, strengthen them against temptation, increase their generosity and their desire to suffer for Christ. Let us "act Christ's love among men and women," remembering the words of the *Imitation of Christ*, "Love feels no burden, values no labours, would willingly do more than it can, complains not of impossibility because it conceives that it may and can do all things; when weary is not tired; when straitened is not constrained, when frightened is not disturbed; but like a lively flame and a torch all on fire, it mounts upwards and securely passes through all oppositions."

*Let me preach you without preaching, not by words but by my example, by the catching force, the sympathetic influence of what I do, the evident fullness of the love my heart bears to you. Amen.*

• There is so much suffering everywhere. Be holy and fervent. God will use you to relieve this suffering. The gospel was preached to the poor to prove that Christ was divine, that he was the expected Messiah. The proof that this is God's work is also that the gospel is preached to the poor. Pray and thank God for having chosen you to live this life and do this work.

• We have been instrumental in preaching the Word of God to the poor, the neglected, the sorrowful, the lonely of all nations. Unworthy though we are, God has used us to make him known and loved by this God-oblivious world. We have the privilege of entering the very homes of the poor and neglected faithful, pulling them and their children out of their beds and bringing them together to praise God in the midst of his Church, to take part in her sacrifice, and to eat the Lord's Supper. What Vatican II has been asking today, we have by the grace of God been already doing since the very moment of foundation of our Society.

• Once, someone asked me, "Why do you go abroad? Don't you have enough poor in India?" So I answered, "I think Jesus told us to go and preach to all the nations." That is why we go all over the world to preach his love and compassion.

**Q:** *Missionaries used to be sent from the supposedly civilized world to the so-called Third World. Now you are coming from India to evangelize us.*
**MT:** It is just what Jesus said, "Go and preach the good news to all nations." Spain is one of the nations where we want to preach. Just as St. Francis Xavier was Spain's gift to India, now India is giving Spain missionaries prepared by St. Francis Xavier, who are returning and proclaiming the Good News. This is a sign of the joy of loving God: sharing that love with others.

• *Converting* means leading to God. *Sanctifying* means filling with God. Converting and sanctifying are God's work. But in his infinite mercy God has chosen the Missionaries of Charity to help him in his own work.

To be able to carry Christ's light to the poorest corners of the slums is a special favor that is granted to us, not due to any special merit on our part. The Missionaries of Charity are willing to devote themselves without rest to search for the dying in the darkest, poorest, and most abandoned places.

Concern is the demonstration of God's true love. Diligence, eagerness, fervor, are the test of love; and the test of fervor is the willingness to devote one's own life to working for souls. We must not feel attached to a single place; we must be willing to go all over the world.

• When speaking is due, we should not be afraid. Someone inside will tell us what we are to say and how we should say it. Christ must be preached in such a way that we can say to pagans that they can get to know him, to heretics and schismatics that they can come back to the right path, to lax Catholics that they can obtain his mercy, and to the good and pious that they can let themselves be consumed by his love.

• The sister must have one thing clear: there is a soul to save, a soul to bring to God. The sister has to be extremely kind and gentle; in touch of hand, in tone of voice, in her smile—for the work is very delicate. Nirmal Hriday (a hospital run by the Missionaries of Charity) is a treasure house; so is every hospital. An unkind word or look is enough to spoil the work. Such perfection of charity is not in us but we must acquire it—kindness in action. You will not learn kindness by looking after sick people unless you practice it on healthy people, because the sick are often trying and hard to please.

• With no opportunity to receive the religious message, the most upright and intelligent spirit is in fact nothing but a bee locked up in a bottle.

• The sisters take care of thousands and thousands of lepers. Our sisters wash lepers covered with wounds, for they are the wounds of Jesus. It is there that we feed Jesus. One day, one of our sisters was lovingly washing a leper's open sores. A Muslim cleric was standing by and watching. He said, "All these years I have believed that Jesus Christ was a prophet. Today I believe that Jesus Christ is God if he is able to give such joy to this sister to do this work with so much love."

• One day, we picked up a man off the street who looked like a fairly well-to-do person. He was completely drunk. He couldn't even stand up because he was so drunk!

We took him to our home. The sisters treated him with such love, such care, such kindness.

After a fortnight, he told the sisters, "Sisters, my heart is open. Through you I have come to realize that God loves me. I've felt his tender love for me. I want to go home." And we helped him get ready to go home.

After a month, he came back to our home and gave the sisters his first paycheck. He told the sisters, "Do to others what you have done to me." And he walked away a different person.

Love had brought him back to his family, to his children's tenderness, to his wife's understanding love.

Let us ask Our Lady to teach us how to love and how to have the courage to share.

• In India, I was asked by some government people, "Don't you want to make us all Christians?"

I said, "Naturally, I would like to give the treasure I have to you, but I cannot. I can only pray for you to have the courage to receive it."

Faith is a gift from God.

• When our sisters were in Ceylon, a minister of state once told me something very surprising. He said, "You know, Mother, I love Christ but I hate Christians." So I asked him how that could be. He answered, "Because Christians do not give us Christ; they do not live their Christian lives to the full." Gandhi said something very similar, "If Christians were to live their Christian lives to the full, there would not be one Hindu left in India." Isn't it very true? This love of Christ should urge us to spend ourselves without ceasing.

• Even God cannot force himself on anyone who does not want him. Faith is a gift. Let us not humiliate the Hindus by saying, "For a plate of rice you give up your religion." Christianity is a living reality. It is a search, and we must desire it and find God.

• Recently, one great Brazilian man, a man of high position, wrote to me that he had lost faith in God and man. He gave up his position and everything and only wanted to commit suicide. One day, as he was passing by a shop, his eyes suddenly fell on a TV in the window. On the TV was the scene of Nirmal Hriday, the sisters looking after the sick and dying. He wrote to me that after seeing that scene, he knelt and prayed for the first time in many years. Now he has decided to turn back to God and have faith in humanity because he saw that God still loves the world.

SIX

# *Blessed Are You Among Women*

In the first chapter of the Gospel of Luke, we read a beautiful story about an angel and a girl. The angel, Gabriel, went on God's errand to a virgin named Mary. "And coming to her, he said, 'Hail, favored one! The Lord is with you.'

"Seeing that Mary was frightened, Gabriel said, 'Do not be afraid, Mary, for you have found favor with God. Behold, you will conceive in your womb and bear a Son, and you shall name him Jesus.'

"But Mary said to the angel, 'How can this be, since I have no relations with a man?'

"And the angel said to her in reply, 'The holy Spirit will come upon you, and the power of the Most High will overshadow you. Therefore the child to be born will be called holy, the Son of God.'

"Mary said, 'Behold, I am the handmaid of the Lord. May it be done to me according to your word.'"

Immediately Mary went to visit her relative Elizabeth, who was pregnant with John the Baptist. "When Elizabeth heard Mary's greeting, the infant leaped in her womb, and Elizabeth, filled with the holy Spirit, cried out in a loud voice and said, 'Most blessed are you among women, and blessed is the fruit of your womb.... Blessed are you who believed that what was spoken to you by the Lord would be fulfilled.'"

This Bible story is the basis for a thousand-year-old prayer, the Hail Mary. It is the main prayer of the rosary, which Mother Teresa and her companions say as they walk through poverty-ridden streets.

Mother Teresa has a deep devotion to the Blessed Virgin, and she often speaks of Mary's obedient response to the angel Gabriel.

*Hail Mary, full of grace! the Lord is with you;*
*blessed are you among women,*
*and blessed is the fruit of your womb, Jesus.*
*Holy Mary, mother of God,*
*pray for us sinners, now*
*and at the hour of our death.*

*Hail Mary, full of grace! the Lord is with you...*

• Many years ago an angel came to bring the good news to Mary. The Prince of Peace was anxious to come to earth and an angel was used to bring the good news that the Creator would become a little child. The Prince of Peace was attracted to a young girl who was a nobody in the eyes of the world. Even the angel could not understand why he was sent to a creature like that. But she was so beautiful that the King of Kings wanted to become flesh in her. She was so full of grace, so pure, so full of God. She looked at the angel—she must have been surprised for she had never seen an angel—and asked, "How? What are you saying? I don't understand what you are saying; it makes no sense to me." And the angel said simply that by the power of the Holy Spirit, Christ would be formed within her. And Mary answered simply: "Behold the handmaid of the Lord."

• No one has learned so well the lesson of humility as Mary did. She, being the handmaid of the Lord, was completely empty of self, and God filled her with grace. "Full of grace" means full of God. A handmaid is at someone's disposal, to be used according to someone's wish with full trust and joy, to belong to someone without reserve. This is one main reason for the spirit of the Society. Total surrender: to be at God's disposal, to be used as it pleases him, to be his handmaid, to belong to him.

• She will teach us her humility: though full of grace—yet only the handmaid of the Lord; though the mother of God—yet serving like a handmaid in the house of Elizabeth; though conceived immaculate—she meets Jesus humiliated, carrying his cross, and near the cross she stands as one of us, as if she were a sinner needing redemption.

Like her, the greater are the graces we have received, let us with greater and more delicate love touch the lepers, the dying, the lonely, the unwanted.

Like her, let us always accept the cross in whatever way it may come.

Humility of the heart of Mary, fill my heart. Teach me as you taught Jesus to be meek and humble of heart and so glorify our Father.

• We read in the Gospel that God loved the world so much that he gave his Son. He gave him to an ordinary, simple, young woman. She was the most pure, the most holy human being. And she on receiving him—knowing who he was—just said, "Humble me. Be done to me according to thy word." What was the word? "Be the mother of Jesus." And that's why I always say, no one in the world could have been a better priest than Mary the most pure. Yet she remained only the handmaid of the Lord. Jesus did not consecrate her.

• See how Our Lady obeyed the angel: "Be it done to me according to thy word." Whose word? The angel's—because he took the place of God. He was sent by God to her. She, the queen of heaven, obeys the angel. See how she obeyed St. Joseph, with what love and submission, without an excuse. To her, St. Joseph was "he" whose place he took.

• The season of Advent is like springtime in nature, when everything is renewed and so is fresh and healthy. Advent is also meant to do this to us—to refresh us and make us healthy, to be able to receive

Christ in whatever form he may come to us. At Christmas he comes as a little child, so small, so helpless, so much in need of his mother and all that a mother's love can give. It was his mother's humility that helped her to do the works of handmaid to Christ—God from God, true God from true God. Let us see and touch the greatness that fills the depths of their humility. We cannot do better than Jesus and Mary. If we really want God to fill us, we must empty ourselves through humility of all that is selfishness in us.

• Let us beg from Our Lady to make our hearts "meek and humble" as her Son's was. It was from her and in her that the heart of Jesus was formed. Let us all try to practice humility and meekness. We learn humility through accepting humiliations cheerfully. Do not let a chance pass you by. It is so very easy to be proud, harsh, moody, and selfish—so easy. But we have been created for greater things; why stoop down to things that will spoil the beauty of our hearts? How much we can learn from Our Lady! She was so humble because she was all for God. She was full of grace. She made use of the almighty power that was in her, the grace of God.

• Let Mary be the cause of our joy. Let each one of us be Jesus to her.

No one learned humility as well as Mary did. She was the slave girl. Being a slave means to be used by all, with joy.

Joy was the Virgin's strength. Only joy could give her the strength to walk without getting tired up to the hill country of Judea in order to carry out a servant's work. We too have to walk without stopping and go beyond the hills of trouble.

• When you look at the inner workings of electrical things, often you see small and big wires, new and old, cheap and expensive lined up. Until the current passes through them there will be no light.

That wire is you and me. The current is God. We have the power to let the current pass through us, use us, produce the light of the world—Jesus. Or we can refuse to be used and allow darkness to spread.

Our Lady was the most wonderful wire. She allowed God to fill her. By her surrender—"Be it done to me according to thy word"—she became "full of grace." The moment she was filled by this current, by the grace of God, she went in haste to Elizabeth's house to connect the wire, John, to the current, Jesus. As his mother said, "This child, John, leaped up with joy at your voice."

Let us ask Our Lady to come into our lives also and make the current, Jesus, use us to go round the world—especially in our own communities so that we can continue connecting the wires of the hearts of men and women with the current, Jesus.

*... blessed are you among women...*

• The silence of the mind and of the heart: Our Lady "kept all these things in her heart." This silence brought her close to our Lord, so that she never had to regret anything. See what she did when St. Joseph was troubled. One word from her would have cleared his mind; she did not say that word, and our Lord himself worked the miracle to clear her name. Would that we could be so convinced of this necessity of silence! I think then the road to close union with God will become very clear.

• Our Lady—the most beautiful among all women, the greatest, the most humble, the purest, the holiest—in the moment when she felt flooded by grace, full of Jesus, ran in haste.

I think this is why God chose a woman to show his love and compassion toward the world. It was she, the woman, who gave evidence of her kindness by immediately sharing what she had just received. To say it in another way, she hastened to share the Eucharist.

As St. Thérèse once said, "I want to place myself in the heart of the church in order to offer love." You and I have been created for that same end: for loving and for that love, as Mary did everywhere and at all times.

We too have to go look for our children, just as Mary did when Jesus was lost. We must live through the worry of not knowing where our children are. The home is not a home without the child.

We also discover the genuine Mary, full of tenderness, in the wedding feast at Cana. She was moved by seeing the newlyweds exposed to the humiliation of not having wine. That is why she said to Jesus, "They have no more wine."

I think this is the wonderful tenderness of a woman's heart: to be aware of the suffering of others and to try to spare them that suffering, as Mary did. Do you and I have that same tenderness in our hearts? Do we have Mary's eyes for discovering the needs of others?

Perhaps in our own homes: Are we able to perceive the needs of our parents, of our husband, of our children? Do our children come home with us, as Jesus went home with Mary his mother? Do we offer our children a home?

We know what happened to Mary, the mother full of tenderness and love who was never ashamed of proclaiming Jesus her Son. Eventually everyone abandoned him. Mary stayed beside him.

Mary was not ashamed by the fact that Jesus was scourged, that his face was spit upon, that he was treated as a leper, as one unwanted, despised, hated by all. Because he was Jesus, her Son. And there surfaced the deep tenderness of her heart as a mother.

Do we know how to stay beside our own in their suffering, in their humiliation? When our husband loses his job, what do we represent to him? Do we feel tenderness toward him? Do we understand his anguish?

When our children are pulled away from us and receive bad advice, do we feel that deep tenderness that makes us go after them in order to draw them toward us, to welcome them kindly in our home, and to love them with all our heart?

Am I like Mary for my sisters in the community? Do I realize their suffering, their sorrows?

If I am a priest, do I have a heart like Mary's? Do I experience the tenderness of forgiveness? Can I offer God's forgiveness to the humbled sinner who stands before me?

• People like to see the sisters accompanied by Mary. With rosary in hand, they are always willing to spread the Good News.

• Through all the work we do for Jesus, with Jesus, to Jesus, we will ask him to deepen our love for his mother, to make it more personal and intimate, so as to—

—love her as he loved her;
—be a cause of joy to her as he was;
—keep close to her as he kept close;
—share with her everything, even the Cross, as he did when she stood near him on Calvary.

• During this time of grace let us, in a special way, ask Our Lady to teach us her silence, her kindness, her humility.

*Silence of Mary speak to me, teach me how with you and like you I can learn to keep all things in my heart as you did, not to answer back when accused or corrected, to pray always in the silence of my heart as you did.*

*... and blessed is the fruit of your womb, Jesus.*

• It is very, very important for us to have a deep love for Our Lady. For she was the one who taught Jesus how to walk, how to pray, how to wash, how to do all the little things that make our human life so beautiful. She had to do them. And the same thing now—she will always be willing to help us and teach us how to be all for Jesus alone, how to love only Jesus, how to touch him and see him, to serve him in the distressing disguise.

• Our vocation is to belong to Jesus. The easiest way and the simplest way of belonging is this: the Holy Spirit makes us do that giving of self, that total surrender to God, without any reflection, without any counting the cost. We call that "blind surrender." It is like Our Lady: When she knew that the Lord was calling, she said Yes. And she never withdrew that Yes. It was a blind, continual Yes in her life. It is the same thing for us. The whole of our life must come to that one word Yes. Yes to God: that is holiness. We allow God to take from us whatever he wants and we accept whatever he gives with joy. That is Yes in action.

• Because God loves the world he sent his Son. Now he sends you to be his word, and that word has to take flesh in the hearts of the people. That's why you need Our Lady; when the Word of God came to her, became flesh in her, then she gave it to others. It is the same for you. The Word of God has come to you and has become flesh in you and then you must be able to give that love.

• Mary in the mystery of her annunciation and visitation is the very model of the way you should live, because first she received Jesus in her life, then she went in haste to give to her cousin Elizabeth; what she had received, she had to give. You must be like her, giving in haste the word you have received in meditation. In every Holy Communion, Jesus the Word becomes flesh in our life, a special, delicate, beautiful gift of God. But you must protect it with tender care because he is giving himself, the Word, to you to be made flesh, to each one of you, and to those who will come after.

• I believe that our mother the Church has elevated women to a great honor in the presence of God by proclaiming Mary the mother of the Church. God so loved the world that he gave his Son. This was the first Eucharist: the gift of his Son, when he gave him to Our Lady, establishing in her the first altar. Mary was, from that instant on, the only one who was able to affirm with complete sincerity, "This is my body." She offered her body, her strength, her whole being, to form the body of Christ.

It was on her that the power of the Holy Spirit rested, and in her that the Word became flesh. Mary gave herself to him completely because she had previously consecrated herself to him—in order to preserve her virginity virgin, her purity pure, and her chastity chaste, and in order to offer them to the only living God.

When the angel announced to Mary the coming of Christ, she only posed a question: She could not understand how she could take back the gift of herself that she had made to God. The angel explained it, and she understood immediately. Her lips uttered a beautiful response that asserted all that she was as a woman: "I am the servant of the Lord. Let it be done to me as you say."

• Mary did not feel ashamed. She proclaimed Jesus her Son. At Calvary we see her standing upright—the mother of God, standing next to the cross.

What a deep faith she must have had because of her love for her Son! To see him dishonored, unloved, an object of hatred. Yet, she stayed upright.

As the mother possesses her son, she possessed him, knowing that he who belonged to her was at the same time her absolute master. She was not afraid to accept him as her belonging.

Do we know how to consider our own as our belonging when they suffer, when they are discarded? Do we acknowledge our own as our family when they suffer? Do we realize the hunger they have for Jesus in the hunger they feel for a love that understands them?

This is the source of Mary's greatness: her understanding love. You and I who are women—do we possess that great and magnificent thing, that love full of understanding?

This is the love I observe with amazement in our people, in the poor women who day after day discover suffering and accept it because of their love for their children. I have seen many fathers and mothers deprive themselves of many things—very many!—and even beg, in order for their children to have what is needed. I have seen fathers affectionately carry their abnormal children in their arms because those children are their own. I have seen mothers full of a very tender love toward their children.

I remember a mother of twelve children, the last of them terribly mutilated. It is impossible for me to describe that creature. I volunteered to welcome the child into our house, where there are many others in similar conditions.

The woman began to cry. "For God's sake, Mother," she said, "don't tell me that. This creature is the greatest gift of God to me and my family. All our love is focused on her. Our lives would be empty if you took her from us."

Hers really was a love full of understanding and tenderness. Do we have a love like that today? Do we realize that our child, our husband, our wife, our father, our mother, our sister or brother, has a need for that understanding, for the warmth of our hand?

• I desire for you the joy of the Virgin, who because she was humble in her heart, was able to keep Jesus in her womb for nine months. What a long communion!

*Holy Mary, mother of God,*
*pray for us sinners, now...*

• Let us beg from Our Lady to make our hearts "meek and humble" like her Son's was. It was from her and in her that the heart of Jesus was formed.

• Let us always ask Our Lady to be with us when we pray together. Our intercessory prayer to Mary, the mother of Jesus, shall be this:

*Give us a heart as beautiful, pure, and spotless as yours. A heart like yours, so full of love and humility. May we be able to receive Jesus as the Bread of Life, to love him as you loved him, to serve him under the mistreated face of the poor. We ask this through Jesus Christ our Lord. Amen.*

• The Magnificat is Our Lady's prayer of thanks. She can help us to love Jesus best; she is the one who can show us the shortest way to Jesus. Mary was the one whose intercession led Jesus to work the first miracle. "They have no wine," she said to Jesus. "Do whatever he tells you," she said to the servants. We take the part of the servants. Let us go to her with great love and trust. We are serving Jesus in the distressing disguise of the poor.

• Ask Jesus to help you to personalize your love for Mary—in order to love as he loves; in order to be sources of joy, as he is; in order to be closer to her, as he is; in order to share with her everything, even the cross.

Every one of us must carry his or her own cross; it is our sign of belonging to Christ. We need Mary to help us share it.

Holiness is not a luxury but a duty. Great holiness is simple if we belong completely to Mary.

We must be very grateful to God for the burdensome trips we

have undertaken in the streets, by train, by plane, by bicycle, in search of souls; for the joy we have tried to spread in the world. Let us give full freedom to the Virgin for her to use us.

• Let us ask Our Lady to keep us company, to stay with us. Let us ask Mary, who besides being the mother of Jesus, is so beautiful, so pure, so immaculate, and full of grace! If Mary stays with us, we can keep Jesus in our hearts, so that we can love and serve him through ministry to the poorest of the poor.

### *... and at the hour of our death.*

• Death is the most decisive moment in human life. It is like our coronation: to die in peace with God.

• The Virgin always protects us. She is the cause of our joy, and we try to be a cause for her joy. Thus gathered, following her example, invoking her protection, staying united with her, we can move through the most difficult places with no fear at all because Jesus is with us and he will never abandon us: Jesus is our love, our strength, our source of kindness.

• At the moment of death we will not be judged by the amount of work we have done but by the weight of love we have put into our work. This love should flow from self-sacrifice, and it must be felt to the point of hurting.

• Death, in the final analysis, is only the easiest and quickest means to go back to God. If only we could make people understand that we come from God and that we have to go back to him!

Everyone knows that we have not been created by ourselves. Someone else has created us. Going back to him is going back home.

We sisters face death almost every day. It is beautiful to see people who die with dignity, radiating joy at going back to the place they came from, at going back to the only One who loves them.

Those who have had many possessions, who have had many goods and riches, are obsessed by them. They think that the only thing that counts is possessing wealth. That is why it is so difficult for them to leave all things. It is much easier for the poor, who are so free, for this freedom allows them to depart with joy.

SEVEN

# *Day by Day*

Seven hundred and fifty years ago, St. Richard of Chichester wrote a prayer that is still remembered and prayed today. A form of it even became popular during the seventies as the song "Day by Day" from the musical *Godspell.*

The prayer's appeal comes from its rhythm and rhyme, but also from its total dedication to Jesus Christ in ***head*** ("know thee more clearly"), ***heart*** ("love thee more dearly"), and ***hand*** ("follow thee more nearly").

This whole-person devotion to the Lord is a hallmark of Mother Teresa's life and sayings. Daily she and her Missionaries of Charity seek a more intimate knowledge of Christ before they follow him into the streets in service to others and again after they return home. They bathe their prayer and their work in love.

***Thanks be to thee, O Lord Jesus Christ, for all the benefits which thou hast given us; for all the pains and insults which thou hast borne for us. O most merciful redeemer, friend and brother, may we know thee more clearly, love thee more dearly, and follow thee more nearly; for thine own sake.***

***Thanks be to thee, O Lord Jesus Christ, for all the benefits which thou hast given us...***

- "Who do you say that I am?" (Mt 16:15):
  You are God.
  You are God from God.

You are begotten not made.
You are one in substance with the Father.
You are the Son of the Living God.
You are the second Person of the Blessed Trinity.
You are One with the Father.
You are in the Father from the beginning.
All things were made by you and the Father.
You are the beloved Son in whom the Father is well pleased.
You are the Son of Mary, conceived by the Holy Spirit in the womb of Mary.
You were born in Bethlehem.
You were wrapped in swaddling clothes by Mary and put in a manger full of straw.
You were kept warm by the breath of the donkey who carried your mother with you in her womb.
You are the Son of Joseph, the carpenter as known by the people of Nazareth.
You are an ordinary man without much learning, as judged by the learned people of Israel.

• Who is Jesus to me?
Jesus is the Word made flesh.
Jesus is the Bread of Life.
Jesus is the Victim offered for our sins on the cross.
Jesus is the sacrifice offered at holy Mass for the sins of the world and for mine.
Jesus is the Word—to be spoken.
Jesus is the truth—to be told.
Jesus is the way—to be walked.
Jesus is the light—to be lit.
Jesus is the life—to be lived.
Jesus is the love—to be loved.
Jesus is the joy—to be shared.
Jesus is the sacrifice—to be offered.
Jesus is the peace—to be given.
Jesus is the Bread of Life—to be eaten.

Jesus is the hungry—to be fed.
Jesus is the thirsty—to be satiated.
Jesus is the naked—to be clothed.
Jesus is the homeless—to be taken in.
Jesus is the sick—to be healed.
Jesus is the lonely—to be loved.
Jesus is the unwanted—to be wanted.
Jesus is the leper—to wash his wounds.
Jesus is the beggar—to give him a smile.
Jesus is the drunkard—to listen to him.
Jesus is the mentally ill—to protect him.
Jesus is the little one—to embrace him.
Jesus is the blind—to lead him.
Jesus is the dumb—to speak for him.
Jesus is the crippled—to walk with him.
Jesus is the drug addict—to befriend him.
Jesus is the prostitute—to remove from danger and befriend her.
Jesus is the prisoner—to be visited.
Jesus is the old—to be served.

• To me:
Jesus is my God.
Jesus is my spouse.
Jesus is my life.
Jesus is my only love.
Jesus is my all in all.
Jesus is my everything.
JESUS, I love with my whole heart, with my whole being.
I have given him all, even my sins, and he has espoused me to himself in all tenderness and love.
Now and for life I am the spouse of my crucified Spouse.

• Today, when everything is questioned and changed, let us go back to Nazareth. Jesus had come to redeem the world, to teach us the love of his Father. How strange that he should spend thirty years just doing nothing, wasting his time! Not giving expression to his personality or to his gifts! We know that at the age of twelve he silenced the learned priests of the Temple, who knew so much and so well. But when his parents found him, he went down to Nazareth and was subject to them. For twenty years we hear no more of him, so that the people were astonished when he came in public to preach. He, a carpenter's son, doing just the humble work in a carpenter's shop for thirty years!

• Some years have gone by but I will never forget a young French girl who came to Calcutta one day.

She looked so worried. She went to work in our home for dying destitutes. Then, after ten days, she came to see me.

She hugged me and said, "I've found Jesus!"

I asked where she found Jesus.

"In the home for dying destitutes," she answered.

"And what did you do after you found him?"

"I went to confession and Holy Communion for the first time in fifteen years."

Then I said again, "What else did you do?"

"I sent my parents a telegram saying that I found Jesus."

I looked at her and I said, "Now, pack up and go home. Go home and give joy, love, and peace to your parents."

She went home radiating joy, because her heart was filled with joy. She went home, and what joy she brought to her family!

Why?

Because she had lost the innocence of her youth and had gotten it back again.

• Let us begin our way of the cross with cheer and joy because through Holy Communion we have Jesus with us. We have Jesus, the Bread of Life, who gives us life and strength. His joy is our strength, and his passion is also our vigor. Without him we can do nothing.

• Let us be like a genuine and fruitful branch of the vine, which is Christ, accepting him in our lives the way he gives himself to us: as truth, which must be spoken; as life, which must be lived; as light, which must shine out; as love, which must be loved; as a way, which must be trodden; as joy, which must be communicated; as peace, which must be radiated; as sacrifice, which must be offered in our families, to our closest neighbors, and to those who live far away.

*... for all the pains and insults which thou hast borne for us.*

• We do not accept poverty because we are forced to be poor but because we choose to be poor for the love of Jesus; because he, being rich, became poor for love of us. Let us not deceive ourselves.

• Jesus, you have died; you have given everything, life, blood, all. Now it is my turn.

The common soldier fights in the ordinary lines, but the devoted one tries to be near the captain to share his fate. This is the only truth, the only thing that matters, for it is the spirit of Christ.

• Each time Jesus wanted to prove his love for us, he was rejected by mankind. Before his birth his parents asked for a simple dwelling place and they were given none because they were poor. The innkeeper probably looked at Joseph the carpenter and decided that he would not be able to pay. So he refused. But Mother Earth opened a cave and took in the Son of God.

Again, before the redemption and the resurrection, Jesus was rejected by his people. They did not want him—they wanted Caesar; they did not want him—they wanted Barabbas. At the end, it was as if his own Father did not want him because he was covered with our sins. In his holiness he cried, "My God, my God why hast thou forsaken me?"

Yesterday is always today to God. Therefore, today in the world Jesus stands covered with our sins, in the distressing disguise of my sister, my brother. Do I want him? If we are not careful, soon the riches of the worldly spirit will become an obstacle. We will not be able to see God, for Jesus has said: "Blessed are the clean of heart, for they shall see God."

People rejected Jesus because his poverty was hurting their riches. My sisters, do our poor reject us because our riches hurt their poverty? Are they at ease with us because we are so like them in poverty? Can we look straight in the face of the poor and say with a sincere heart: "I know poverty; she is my companion: I love poverty; she is my mother." "I serve poverty; she is my mistress."

• When he showed his heart to St. Margaret Mary, Jesus said again and again, "Love me as I have loved you." "Impossible," she said, "the only way I can do it is if you take my heart and give me yours." Let us ask Jesus sincerely, "Let me share your loneliness, your being unloved, uncared for." Do something today to share in the passion. Maybe Jesus is asking something of you in a special way, maybe something small. If he is not asking you, it might be because you are holding very tightly to something. He will never force it out of you. Maybe he wants you just to smile, to say "May I," to be on time, or to give up an unhealthy friendship.

• Even though he no longer needs to take up his cross and walk toward Calvary, today—in you, in me, in the youth of our world—Jesus continues to endure his passion. The small child, the child full of hunger who eats his bread crumb by crumb because he is afraid of running out of bread before running out of hunger—that is the first station of the cross.

• Today small beings are deprived of love even before birth. They have to die because we do not want one more child. That child has to be left naked because we do not want him. Jesus bore that unspeakable suffering. This unborn child bears it because no other possibility is offered him. But I can want him, love him, care for him. This child is my brother, my sister.

• It is good for us to focus on our Lord and ask ourselves, "Do I really love Jesus like that? Do I really accept the joy of loving by sharing in his passion?" Because even today Jesus is looking for somebody to console and comfort him.

You remember what happened in Gethsemane: Jesus was longing for somebody to share in his agony. The same thing happens in our lives. Can he share his sorrow with us? Are you there to comfort him?

He comes to you in the hungry.
He comes to you in the naked.
He comes to you in the lonely.
He comes to you in the drunkard.
He comes to you in the prostitute.
He comes to you in the street person.
He may come to you in the lonely father, or mother, or sister, or brother in your own family.
Are you willing to share the joy of his love with them?

• I have the impression that the passion of Christ is being relived everywhere. Are we willing to share in this passion? Are we willing to share people's sufferings, not only in poor countries but all over the world?

It seems to me that this great poverty of suffering in the West is much harder to solve. When I pick up some starving person off the street and offer him a bowl of rice or a piece of bread, I can satisfy his hunger. But a person that has been beaten or feels unwanted or unloved or fearful or rejected by society—that person experiences a kind of poverty that is much more painful and deep. Its cure is much more difficult to find. Our sisters work among these kinds of people in the West. They share in the passion of Christ.

• Let's fix our eyes on the cross. What do we see? We see his head bent down to kiss us. Look at his hands. They say, "I love you!" We see his arms stretched out on the cross as if to embrace us. We see his heart opened wide to receive us. That is the cross, which is represented by the crucifix that most of us have in our homes. Each time we glance at it, it should help us to fall in love with Christ. It should help us to love him with sincerity of heart. What greater love is there than God's love for each one of us? His love isn't a fantasy. It is real.

*O most merciful redeemer, friend, and brother,*
*may we know thee more clearly...*

• We have to possess before we can give. He who has the mission of giving to others must grow first in the knowledge of God. He must be full of that knowledge.

• Knowledge will make you strong as death. Love Jesus generously. Love him trustfully, without looking back and without fear. Give yourself fully to Jesus—he will use you to accomplish great things on the condition that you believe much more in his love than in your weakness. Believe in him—trust in him with blind and absolute confidence because he is Jesus. Believe that Jesus and Jesus alone is life—and sanctity is nothing but that same Jesus intimately living in you; then his hand will be free with you. Give yourself unswervingly, conforming yourself in all things to his holy will which is made known to you through your superior.

• If day after day we devote ourselves to the perfect fulfillment of our spiritual duties, he will gradually admit us to a closer intimacy so that even outside the time dedicated to prayer we shall find no difficulty in remaining conscious of the divine presence. On the other hand, the diligent practice of the presence of God by means of fervent aspirations in our labors and in our recreations will be rewarded with more abundant graces. We must endeavor to live alone with Jesus in the sanctuary of our inmost heart.

• From the moment a soul has the grace to know God, he must seek. If he does not seek, he is going astray from the just way. God offers all souls created by him an opportunity to meet him face-to-face, to accept him or to reject him.

• The aim of taking a retreat is to advance in the knowledge and love of God, to purify ourselves, and to reform and transform our lives according to the life of our model, Jesus Christ. It is a time of greater silence, of more fervent prayer, of special penance, and more intense spiritual activity. It is not so much a looking back on the achievements and failure of the past, as a looking forward to a more generous imitation of our Lord himself.

• Jesus must be brought to every man and woman. Jesus is the only answer. You, as Co-workers, must be free yourselves. If you use the name "Mother Teresa" in your work, that is only because it is a means to serving and loving Christ in the poor. In the bottom of your heart, you must be convinced that you and I are together co-workers of Christ. As such, you must be very close to him. You must share with him. You must be at his complete disposal.

The last time we had a meeting of Co-worker coordinators in the United States, I told them, "Every Co-worker must be at Christ's disposal to such a degree that Christ can make use of him without having to ask, May I? Can't I? Will you allow me? In other words, without previous consent."

It is something very beautiful and freeing to be able to give ourselves fully to Jesus, each of us in our own way, each one of us in our own family."

• Christ has chosen you so that you will be able to live out precisely this great vocation: your loving vocation as Co-workers. Why you and not others? Why me and not others? I do not know; it is a mystery. But being together should help us to deepen our knowledge of God, and that knowledge will lead us to love him, and love will lead us to serve him.

• The simplicity aspect of our life of contemplation makes us see the face of God in everything, everyone, everywhere, all the time, and his hand in all the happenings, and makes us do all that we do—whether we think, study, work, speak, eat, or take our rest—in Jesus, with Jesus, for Jesus and to Jesus, under the loving gaze of the Father, being totally available to him in any form he may come to us.

• Jesus, in the least of his brethren, is not only hungry for a piece of bread, but hungry for love, to be known, to be taken into account.

• Jesus said, "Learn of me." In our meditations we should always say, "Jesus, make me a saint according to your own heart, meek and humble." We must respond in the spirit in which Jesus meant us to respond. We know him better now, through meditations, and the study of the gospel, but have we really understood him in his humility? Does this humility appeal to us, attract us?

• I remember one of our sisters, who had just graduated from the university. She came from a well-to-do family that lived outside of India.

According to our rule, the very next day after joining our society, the postulants must go to the home for dying destitutes in Calcutta. Before this sister went, I told her, "You saw the priest during the Mass, with what love, with what delicate care he touched the body of Christ. Make sure you do the same thing when you get to the home, because Jesus is there in a distressing disguise."

So she went, and after three hours, she came back. That girl from the university, who had seen and understood so many things, came to my room with such a beautiful smile on her face. She said, "For three hours I've been touching the body of Christ!"

And I said, "What did you do? What happened?"

She said, "They brought a man from the street who had fallen into a drain and had been there for some time. He was covered with maggots and dirt and wounds. And though I found it very difficult, I cleaned him, and I knew I was touching the body of Christ!"

She knew!

Do we know?

Do we recognize Jesus under the appearance of bread?

If we recognize him under the appearance of bread, we will have no difficulty recognizing him in the disguise of the suffering poor, and the suffering in our family, in our own community.

*... love thee more dearly...*

• Love Jesus with a big heart. Serve Jesus with joy and gladness of spirit, casting aside and forgetting all that troubles and worries you. To be able to do all these, pray lovingly like children, with an earnest desire to love much.

• I think I'm not afraid for you brothers if you deepen your personal love for Christ. Then you will be all right. Then people may pass you by, but you will not be hurt, you will not be harmed. The first time you go out they may throw stones at you, all right. Turn the other side—let them throw at the other side also; what is important is that you are holding on, that you have got a grip on Christ and he will not let your hand go.

• How can I love Jesus whom I do not see if I don't love my sister or brother—or the poor—whom I do see? If I do not, St. John says: "You are a liar."

• Never lose the chance to become like Jesus. We profess before the world, "I am the spouse of Jesus crucified." Like the woman at the altar who professes before the world her marriage to one man, we, too, change our name to show that we belong to Jesus completely.

• The child is the fruit of married love. How beautiful! God has said: "Let man and woman be created for that purpose."

The church is the spouse of Jesus, and for us Missionaries of Charity the fruit of that oneness with Jesus is the poor. Just as the fruit of mother and father is the child, so the fruit of my relationship with Jesus and me is the poor.

Today ask yourself: "What is the fruit of my vow of chastity?"

• Our Lord has a very special love for the chaste. His own mother, St. Joseph, and St. John the beloved disciple all were consecrated to chastity. Why do I desire to be chaste? I want to be chaste because I am the spouse of Jesus Christ, the Son of the living God. I want to be chaste because of the work I have to do as the co-worker of Christ. My chastity must be so pure as to draw the most impure to the Sacred Heart of Jesus.

• What is our spiritual life? A love union with Jesus, in which the divine and the human give themselves completely to one another. All that Jesus asks of me is to give myself to him in all poverty and nothingness.

• I want you all to fill your hearts with great love. Don't imagine that love, to be true and burning, must be extraordinary. No; what we need in our love is the continuous desire to love the One we love.

• I will never forget one day in Venezuela when I went to visit a family who had given us a lamb. I went to thank them and there I found out that they had a badly crippled child.

I asked the mother, "What is the child's name? What do you call him at home?"

The mother gave me a most beautiful answer. "We call him 'Teacher of Love,' because he keeps on teaching us how to love. Everything we do for him is our love for God in action."

What a beautiful spirit!

• There is such a beautiful thing in India—the red dot on the forehead. The meaning for the Hindu is that his whole thought and attention, everything must be concentrated on God. For the married woman it is the same. The red marking along the part in her hair means that all her thoughts are for her husband. We, too, must be fully for Jesus, giving him that undivided love.

• By the vow of chastity, I not only renounce the married state of life, but I also consecrate to God the free use of my internal and external acts—my affections. I cannot in conscience love a creature with the love of a woman for a man. I no longer have the right to give that affection to any other creature but only to God. What, then? Do we have to be stones, human beings without hearts? Do we simply say: "I don't care; to me all human beings are the same." No, not at all. We have to keep ourselves as we are, but keep it all for God, to whom we have consecrated all our external and internal acts.

• Chastity does not simply mean that we are not married. It means that we love Christ with an undivided love. It is not only that we cannot have a family, we cannot get married. But it is something deeper, something living, something real—it is to love him with undivided, loving chastity through the freedom of poverty.

We must be free to love—and to love him with an undivided love. Nothing will separate us from the love of Christ—and that is our vow of chastity.

By this vow we are bound to remain faithful to the humble works of the society: to the poorest of the poor, the unwanted, the unloved, the uncared for. That means we depend solely on Divine Providence.

• What am I binding myself to? What is my vow to God about?—I bind myself to God with undivided love. I tell Almighty God, "I can love all, but the only one I will love in particular is you, only you."

• He has chosen us; we have not first chosen him. But we must respond by making our Society something beautiful for God—something very beautiful. For this we must give all—our utmost. We must cling to Jesus, grasp him, have a grip on him, and never let go for anything. We must fall in love with Jesus.

*... and follow thee more nearly; for thine own sake.*

• Knowledge of God, love of God, service of God—that is the end of our lives—and obedience gives us the key to it all.

• Jesus told us, "If you want to be my disciples, take up my cross and follow me" (see Luke 14:27). He meant that we should carry the cross and feed him in those who are hungry; that we should clothe him in those who are naked; that we should host him in our home, treating him as a brother.

• One thing Jesus asks of me: that I lean on him; that in him and only in him I put complete trust; that I surrender myself to him unreservedly. Even when all goes wrong and I feel as if I am a ship without a compass, I must give myself completely to him. I must not attempt to control God's action; I must not count the stages in the journey he would have me make. I must not desire a clear perception of my advance upon the road, must not know precisely where I am upon the way of holiness. I ask him to make a saint of me, yet I must leave to him the choice of the saintliness itself and still more the means which leads to it.

• Jesus is the Light.
Jesus is the Truth.
Jesus is the Life.
We too must be
the Light of Charity
the Truth of Humility
the Life of Sanctity

• What is contemplation? To live the life of Jesus. This is what I understand—to love Jesus, to live his life in us, to live our life in his life. That's contemplation. We must have a clean heart to be able to see: no jealousy, anger, contention, and especially no uncharitableness. To me, contemplation is not to be shut up in a dark place, but to allow Jesus to live his passion, his love, his humility in us, praying with us, being with us, sanctifying through us.

• We must not be afraid to proclaim Christ's love and to love as he loved. In the work we have to do—it does not matter how small and humble it may be—make it Christ's love in action. Do not be afraid to keep a clean and undivided heart and to radiate the joy of being the spouse of Christ crucified. Do not be afraid to go down with Christ and be subject to those who have authority from above and who therefore declare Christ's obedience unto death. Rejoice that one more Christ is walking through the world in you and through you going about doing good.

• Our vocation is to follow the lowliness of Christ. We remain right on the ground by living Christ's concern for the poorest and the lowliest and by being of immediate but effective service to them until they find some others who can help in a better and more lasting way.

• Only by getting closer and closer to Jesus will we be able to get closer to each other and to the poor.

• Every sister and brother ought to grow in the likeness of Christ so that Christ may live his life of compassion and humility in today's world.

• Am I able to see the poor and suffering? We often look without seeing. All of us have to carry our own cross, all of us have to accompany Jesus in his ascent to Calvary if we want to reach the summit with him.

In our way of the cross we see Jesus, poor and hungry, enduring his own falls. Are we there to offer him our help? Are we there with our sacrifices, with our piece of bread, of real bread?

There are thousands of people dying for a piece of bread. There are thousands upon thousands who die for a little bit of love, for a little bit of acknowledgment. This is one station of the cross: Jesus present in those who are hungry and falling under the weight of the cross.

• Simon of Cyrene began following Jesus when he helped him bear his cross. That is what you young people have done throughout this year as a symbol of your love: thousands and thousands of things you have offered Jesus in the poor. You have been genuine Cyrenians each time you have carried out one such action or gesture.

• We must do better than the people in the world, because we do it for Jesus. If we find it difficult, we should ask Jesus to give us a drop from his Precious Blood.

There is a story of a little robin. He saw Jesus on the cross, saw the crown of thorns. The bird flew around and around until he found a way to remove a thorn—and in removing the thorn it stuck him. Each one of us should be that bird. What have I done; what comfort have I given? Does my work really mean something?

The little robin tried to remove just one thorn. When I look at the cross, I think of that robin. Don't pass by the cross—it is a place of grace. The cross—hands seared with pain. Did I put compassion in my hands for one who was sick? How did I touch my patient?

• Pray and work daily that all may become followers of Christ.

• The more united we are to God, the greater will be our love and readiness to serve the poor wholeheartedly. Much depends on this union of hearts. The love of God the Father for the Son, and of the Son for the Father, produces God the Holy Spirit. So also the love of God for us and our love for God should produce this wholehearted, free service for the poor.

# PART THREE

## *Prayers for Our Daily Bread*

Every morning Mother Teresa and her Missionaries of Charity, along with millions of Christians around the world, worship the Lord in the Eucharist. *Eucharist*, a Greek word meaning "thanksgiving," reminds worshipers that when Jesus broke bread with his disciples, he gave thanks. It also encourages them to give thanks to God for the gift of Jesus' love. Christians believe that Jesus is really present with them in a special way whenever they celebrate the Eucharist.

During the Liturgy of the Eucharist, gifts of bread and wine are brought to the altar, and the priest and people pray that the offering will be acceptable. The people sing praise to God's holiness. The priest leads the Eucharistic Prayer, repeating the words Jesus said at the Last Supper and, with all the worshipers, proclaiming faith in Christ who died, is risen, and will come again. When the Eucharistic Prayer is concluded, the people stand and say the Lord's Prayer together. The priest then breaks the bread, announces the presence of the Lamb of God, and calls the people to Communion.

The Eucharist is a vital part of Mother Teresa's prayer life. Part Three is based on several prayers from the Liturgy of the Eucharist that she says and lives every day.

# EIGHT

## *An Acceptable Sacrifice*

Sacrifice is at the heart of Christian faith. The people of God in Old Testament times offered animal sacrifices for their sins—lambs, goats, bulls, and pigeons. Jesus offered himself as a perfect, final sacrifice so that the animal sacrifices would not have to be repeated.

In the sacrifice of the Mass, Jesus feeds his people with his own Body so that they become one with him—so that they, like the bread, can be called the body of Christ. Once Christians understand that they are the body of Christ on earth, they hear Christ calling them to self-sacrifice, to surrender, to suffer on behalf of others. As Christ's body, they will do his work in his way, by giving themselves for others.

Sacrifice, surrender, and suffering are not popular topics nowadays. Our culture makes us believe that we can have it all, that we should demand our rights, that with the right technology all pain and problems can be overcome. This is not the attitude of the Bible, nor is it the attitude of Mother Teresa. The Bible assumes that Jesus' followers will make sacrifices and will suffer, just as Jesus himself did. Mother Teresa knows that it is impossible to relieve the world's suffering unless God's people are willing to surrender to God, to make sacrifices, and to suffer along with the poor.

During the Mass, the priest and the people pray that the sacrifice of bread and wine will be acceptable to God, "for the praise and glory of his name, for our good, and the good of all his church." What is an acceptable sacrifice? One that brings praise and glory to God's name. One that is good for the people of God. One that is made on behalf of the world. This is the kind of sacrifice St. Paul encouraged all believers to make: "I beg you through the mercy of God to offer your bodies as a living sacrifice holy and acceptable to God, your spiritual worship" (Rom 12:1).

• From the beginning of time the human heart has felt the need to offer God a sacrifice, but as St. Paul says, "It was impossible for sins to be taken away by the blood of bulls and goats" (see Hebrews 10:4). Therefore, Jesus Christ had to offer another sacrifice, that of himself: Jesus dying on the cross is our sacrifice. Let us not think that the holy Mass is only a memorial. No, it is the same sacrifice as that which he offered on the cross. It is very consoling that this sacrifice is our sacrifice.

• Lent is a time when we relive the passion of Christ. Let it not be just a time when our feelings are roused, but let it be a change that comes through cooperation with God's grace in real sacrifices of self. Sacrifice, to be real, must cost; it must hurt; it must empty us of self. Let us go through the passion of Christ day by day.

• To resolve to be a saint costs much. Renunciations, temptations, struggles, persecutions, and all kinds of sacrifices surround the resolute soul. One can love God only at one's own expense.

• Try to increase your love for the holy Mass and the passion of Christ by accepting with joy all the little sacrifices that come daily. Do not pass by the small gifts, for they are very precious for yourself and for others.

• If we join the Community outside our own country, or are sent on a mission, we shall freely choose to be there, happy to suffer and die with the people if need arises, and ready to remain there till obedience calls us back. In adapting ourselves to the standard of living of the people among whom we are, we shall sacrifice what is not strictly necessary for our life, remembering that we are relating not just to the poor of that country but to the poor of the whole world.

• Sacrifice, in order to be genuine, has to empty us of ourselves.

• The Co-workers acknowledge that all the goods of this world are free gifts of God and that no one has a right to superfluous wealth as long as there are some who are starving. Co-workers try to make up for this serious injustice by sacrificing luxury in their daily lives.

• It is the young people who will build the world of tomorrow. Today's youth are looking for the challenge of self-denial. A young man from a rich family in New York came in his car to our residence and told me, "I have given everything to the poor, and I have come to follow Christ."

• Jesus has chosen each one of us to be his love and his light in the world. The spirit of sacrifice will always be the salt of our Society.

• There are lonely people around you in hospitals and psychiatric wards. There are so many people that are homeless! In New York, our sisters are working among the destitute who are dying. What pain it causes to see these people! They are only known by their street address now. Yet they were all someone's children. Someone loved them at one time. They loved others during their lifetime. But now they are only known by their street address.

• The words of Jesus, "Love one another as I have loved you," (Jn 15:12, RSV) must be not only a light for us but a flame that consumes the self in us. Love, in order to survive, must be nourished by sacrifices, especially the sacrifice of self.

• Our sisters and brothers have surrendered their lives to the love of Christ, with an undivided love through chastity and the freedom of poverty. For us poverty is a necessity. We have to know what poverty is in order to be able to understand the poor. That is why we need the freedom to be poor with our total surrender through obedience.

• Surrender is also true love. The more we surrender, the more we love God and souls. If we really love souls, we must be ready to take their place, to take their sins upon us and expiate them in us by penance and continual mortification. We must be living holocausts, for the souls need us as such.

• "We are in exile from the Lord's presence as long as we are at home in the body and still desire the things of this world" (St. Francis of Assisi). No contemplation is possible without asceticism and self-abnegation. "The road to God demands one thing necessary: True self denial, exterior and interior, through surrender of self both to suffering for Christ and to annihilation in all things" (St. John of the Cross).

• Total surrender—for us, contemplative life means also a joyous and ardent response to his call to the most intimate union with him by

— totally abandoning ourselves into his hands;
— yielding totally to his every movement of love, giving him supreme freedom over us to express his love as he pleases, with no thought of self;
— desiring with ardent desire all the pain and delight involved in that union.

It also means—

— to be a willing prisoner of his love, a willing victim of his wounded love, a living holocaust;
— even if he cuts us to pieces, to cry out, "Every piece is yours."

• Renouncing means to offer my free will, my reason, my life, in an attitude of faith. My soul can be in darkness; trials are the surest tests of my blind renunciation.

Renunciation also means love. The more we renounce, the more we love God and man.

God's love has no limits. Its depth is unfathomable: "I will not leave you orphaned" (Jn 14:18).

Let's turn the image around. There should also be no limits to the love that impels us to give ourselves over to God and to become victims of his love. The common and ordinary cannot be enough for us. That which is good for others is not enough for us. We have to quench God's thirst by dying for love. Not content with the common good, but with a courage that will face all dangers with a serene soul, willing at all times to make any sacrifice, to accomplish any task or work, the Missionary of Charity must at all times be committed to be as close as possible to her king who is dying of thirst.

• St. Thérèse, the Little Flower, explained surrender very beautifully when she said, "I am like a little ball in the hand of Jesus. He plays with me. He throws me away, puts me in the corner. And then like a little child who wants to see what is inside, he tears the ball apart and throws the pieces away." This is what a brother, a sister, has to be, that little ball in the hand of Jesus, who says to Jesus, "You can do whatever you want, as you want, when you want, as long as you want."

• We are at his disposal. If he wants you to be sick in bed, if he wants you to proclaim his Word in the street, if he wants you to clean the toilets all day, that's all right, everything is all right. We must say, "I belong to you. You can do whatever you like." This is our strength, and this is the joy of the Lord.

• We must know exactly when we say yes to God what is in that yes. Yes means "I surrender," totally, fully, without any counting the cost, without any examination, "Is it all right? Is it convenient?" Our yes to God is without any reservations. That's what it is to be a contemplative. I belong to him so totally that there are no reservations. It doesn't matter what we feel.

• It must have been so hard to have been scourged, to have been spat upon. "Take it away," Jesus prayed during his agony. His Father didn't come to him directly and say, "This is my beloved Son," but he consoled him through an angel. Let us pray that we will fill our hearts with Jesus' surrender, that we will understand total surrender.

• Faith in action through prayer, faith in action through service: each is the same thing, the same love, the same compassion. We all have to proclaim that faith, both the sisters and the brothers. This is something that should encourage us and should be a strength for us, that we complete each other more fully. Because we are human beings, we need this distinction, this separation, these different names. The soul, the mind, and the heart, however, have the same thing: total surrender to God. At the moment we realize that we have really done that, then we are at his disposal, and there are no more differences.

• By the vow of chastity we give up our hearts to our Lord, to the crucified Christ; the one place in our hearts belongs to him.

In the Gospels, we read that God is like a jealous lover. We cannot have two masters, for we will serve one and hate the other.

The vows themselves are but means of leading the soul to God, and the vow of chastity in particular is intended as a means of giving the heart to God. The heart is one of the highest and noblest of the faculties, but it is also a source of danger. By our vow we consecrate our heart to God and renounce the joys of family life.

Yes, we do renounce the natural gift of God to women to become mothers for the greater gift, that of being virgins of Christ, of becoming mothers of souls.

• Total abandonment consists of giving oneself fully to God because God has given himself to us. If God, who owes us nothing, is willing to give us nothing less than himself, can we respond by giving him only a part of ourselves? Renouncing myself, I give myself to God that he might live in me.

How poor we would be if God had not given us the power to give ourselves over to him! Instead, how rich we are right now!

How easy it is to conquer God! We give ourselves to him, and God becomes ours, and now we have nothing but God. The prize with which God rewards our self-abandonment is himself.

• Our total surrender to God means to be entirely at the disposal of the Father as Jesus and Mary were. In giving ourselves completely to

God, because God has given himself to us, we are entirely at his disposal—

- — to be possessed by him so that we may possess him;
- — to take whatever he gives and to give whatever he takes with a big smile;
- — to be used by him as it pleases him without being consulted;
- — to offer him our free will, our reason, our whole life in pure faith, so that he may think his thoughts in our minds, do his work through our hands, and love with our hearts.

• We should not be concerned with the instrument God uses to speak to us, but with what God is saying to us. Let us pray to understand what it means to be at his disposal.

• Once the Cardinal of St. Louis asked me to write something for him in his breviary. I wrote, "Let Jesus use you without consulting you." He wrote back, "You don't know what you have done to me. I examine my conscience every day and ask, 'Did I allow Jesus to use me without consulting me?'"

• God has been pouring many graces into the congregation, and I think we owe deep gratitude to the poor. Their life of suffering, their life of prayer, their life of tremendous forbearance obtains many graces for us. Also, there are all those thousands of people who have died in our hands. I am sure they pray much for us when they go to heaven. The whole thing is nothing extraordinary, nothing special. It has been just a simple surrender, a simple yes to Christ, allowing him to do what he wants. That is why the work is his work. I'm just a little pencil in his hand. Tomorrow, if he finds somebody more helpless, more stupid, more hopeless, I think he will do still greater things with her and through her.

• Suffering has to come because if you look at the cross, he has got his head bending down—he wants to kiss you—and he has both hands open wide—he wants to embrace you. He has his heart opened wide to receive you. Then when you feel miserable inside, look at the cross and you will know what is happening. Suffering is a gift from God. It is between you and Jesus alone inside. Suffering, pain, sorrow, humiliation, feelings of loneliness, are nothing but the kiss of Jesus, a sign that you have come so close that he can kiss you.

• I fulfill what is wanting in the passion of Christ. It is very difficult to understand what the connection is between our penances and the passion of Christ. We must constantly follow in the footsteps of Jesus Christ and in a certain manner crucify our own flesh.

• Remember that the passion of Christ ends always in the joy of the resurrection of Christ, so when you feel in your own heart the suffering of Christ, remember the resurrection has to come, the joy of Easter has to dawn. Never let anything so fill you with sorrow as to make you forget the joy of Christ risen.

• My dear children, without our suffering, our work would just be social work, very good and helpful, but not the work of Jesus Christ, not part of the redemption. Jesus wanted to help us by sharing our life, our loneliness, our agony, and our death. All that he has taken on himself, and has carried it into the darkest night; only by being one with us has he redeemed us. We are allowed to do the same; all the desolation of the poor people, not only their material poverty but also their spiritual destitution, must be redeemed and we must share in it.

• The incurably ill can become very close co-workers to a Missionary of Charity by offering their suffering for that sister or brother. Every sister and brother can thus have a second self to pray and suffer for her or for him. Everyone will draw from this support a new strength, and their lives will be like the burning lamp that wastes away for the sake of souls.

• Suffering is nothing by itself, but suffering that is shared with the passion of Christ is a wonderful gift and a sign of love. God is very good to give you so much suffering and so much love. All this becomes for me a real joy, and it gives me great strength because of you.

It is your life of sacrifice that gives me so much strength. Your prayers and suffering are like the chalice in which those of us who work can pour the love of the souls we encounter. So you are just as necessary as we are. We and you together can do all things in him who strengthens us.

How beautiful is your vocation of suffering Co-workers: you are messengers of God's love. We carry in our hearts the love of God, who is thirsty for souls; you can quench his thirst through your incomparable suffering, to which our hard work is united. It is you who have tasted the chalice of his agony.

• We often say to Christ, "Make us partakers of your suffering." But, when someone is insensitive to us, how easily we forget that this is the moment to share with Christ! It would be enough for us to remember that it is Jesus who gives us, through such a person or circumstance, the opportunity to do something beautiful for him.

• Suffering is nothing by itself. But suffering shared with the passion of Christ is a wonderful gift, the most beautiful gift, a token of love. By giving up his Son, the Father has given the world a token of his love. It was a gift, the greatest gift of love, for his suffering was his expiation for sin.

• We have to suffer with Christ. In doing this we will share in the sufferings of the poor.

Our congregation may die if the sisters do not walk in Christ's rhythm in his suffering and if they do not live in poverty. Our rigorous poverty is our safeguard. We do not want, as has been the case with other religious orders throughout history, to begin serving the poor and then gradually move toward serving the rich.

In order for us to understand and to be able to help those who lack everything, we have to live as they live. The difference lies only in the fact that those we aid are poor by force, whereas we are poor by choice.

• My thoughts often run to you who suffer, and I offer your sufferings which are so great while mine are so small.

Those of you who are sick, when things are hard, take refuge in Christ's heart. There my own heart will find with you strength and love.

Do you desire to suffer with a pure love? Do it with the love that Christ has chosen for you. Give more and more, until you have given everything.

How grateful I am that God has given you to me! My soul is encouraged by the thought that you are offering your prayers and pains for our work's sake. This makes my smile come more easily.

You suffer, we work. You and we together are offering the same chalice.

• In order for us to become saints we will have to suffer a great deal. Suffering begets love and life in souls.

As messengers of God's love, how full of love we are to be in order to be faithful to our name! Let us remain with Mary beside the crucified Jesus, with our chalice made up of the four vows and full of the wine of our own sacrifice.

All of our gestures should be aimed at increasing our own perfection and that of our neighbor—offering our care to the sick and to the dying, picking up and educating children who are abandoned in the streets, offering shelter to the dispossessed. Devoting oneself to the conversion of the poor in the inner city is an arduous and restless task, with no results and no reward.

• (To sick Co-workers) How happy I feel because of you! Often, when my work is very hard, I think about you and say to Jesus, "Look at these children of yours who suffer, and bless my work for their sake." I feel instantly comforted. You see, you are our hidden treasure, the secret strength of the Missionaries of Charity. I personally feel very happy, and a new strength comes over my soul, as I think of all those who are spiritually united to us. With your collaboration and help, what won't we be able to accomplish for him!

• Recently a real windfall of charity was experienced throughout Bengal. Food and clothing arrived from everywhere. It came from schools, men, women, and children to be distributed during the recent monsoon disaster. The monsoon was something terrible, but it brought about something very beautiful. It brought about sharing. It brought about the concern and awareness that our brothers and sisters were suffering because of a natural disaster. And many people decided to do something to help them. There were people who prepared meals in their homes to share with those in need. It was something very beautiful to witness that such terrible suffering could help bring about so much good in so many people.

**Q:** *How can we believe in a good God when there is so much suffering around us?*

**MT:** Suffering in and of itself is useless, but suffering which is a share in the passion of Christ is a marvelous gift for human life. The most wonderful of gifts is that we can share in Christ's passion.

**Q:** *How? Is suffering a gift?*

**MT:** Yes, and it is a sign of love because it was chosen by the Father to show us that he loved the world by giving up his Son to die for us. In that way, through Christ's life, suffering proved to be a gift, the greatest gift of love, because through his suffering our sins were atoned for.

**Q:** *Our sins?*

**MT:** Yes, above all, our sins. That's why we come back to the same thing. If we admit that we are sinners and we need forgiveness, then it will be very easy for us to forgive others. But if I don't admit this, it will be very hard for me to say, "I forgive you" no matter who comes to me.

**Q:** *What should we do when suffering comes to us?*

**MT:** Accept it with a smile.

**Q:** *Accept it with a smile?*

**MT:** Yes, with a smile, because it is the greatest gift that God gives us.

• To become a saint one must suffer much, and to love much we must suffer more. Suffering begets love, but it is also fruitful because it begets life for souls. How full of love we must be in order to be true to our name.

• "My child, receive the symbol of our crucified spouse. Follow his footsteps in search of souls. Carry him and his light into the homes of the poor, especially to the souls most in need. Spread the charity of his heart wherever you go and so satisfy his thirst for souls."

These words express beautifully the whole of our life. If we just live this, we will be holy; we will be spouses of Jesus crucified.

Suffering will come, trouble will come—that's part of life—a sign that you are alive. If you have no suffering and no trouble, the devil is taking it easy. You are in his hand.

If I am the spouse of Jesus crucified, he has to kiss me. Naturally, the nails will hurt me. If I come close to the crown of thorns, it will hurt me. If a man leaves his father and mother and clings to his wife, they become one. They cleave to each other. If I am one with Jesus, it must hurt when I share his sorrow.

# NINE

## *Holy, Holy, Holy Lord*

People often refer to Mother Teresa as a saint. In one sense, she is not a saint—the church officially gives that title to a select number of holy people after much careful study, and Mother Teresa's life has not yet been reviewed. In another sense, though, she is definitely a saint—as are all Christians. In the New Testament, Jesus' followers are often called saints ("holy ones").

Holiness, or sanctity, is a constant theme of Mother Teresa's. To become holy is to become like God.

Long ago human beings were created like God, "in the divine image" (Gn 1:27). But sin intervened and distorted the image. In order for the image to shine forth clearly again, it would be necessary to remove sin. This is why Jesus Christ died and rose from the dead, and this is why God sent the Holy Spirit to his people.

God, in his love for the human race, calls us to him so that we may "share the image of his Son" (Rom 8:29). He wants to make us holy, to sanctify us, to make us like God. This holiness is not given to us magically. We become more and more like God as we spend our lives with him, listening to him, learning his will, and doing his work on earth.

Every day at Mass, Mother Teresa and the Missionaries of Charity sing a hymn of praise to God's holiness. The hymn was already ancient in Jesus' day. The first part is taken from Isaiah's words when he had a vision of God in the temple (see Isaiah 6:3); the second part comes from Psalm 118.

The Christian hymn is sometimes called the *Sanctus*, from the Latin word for "holy." It was sung in the East from the earliest days of Christianity and came to the West no later than the fifth century. During the Middle Ages, when most church music was sung by choirs, the people still sang the Sanctus. It is appropriate that Mother Teresa's missionaries begin each day singing about God's holiness, before they go out into the world as holy people, doing God's work on earth, restoring the divine image in humanity.

*Holy, holy, holy Lord, God of power and might,*
*Heaven and earth are full of your glory.*
*Hosanna in the highest.*
*Blessed is he who comes in the name of the Lord.*
*Hosanna in the highest.*

• Let us thank God for all his love for us, in so many ways and in so many places. Let us in return, as an act of gratitude and adoration, determine to be holy because he is holy.

• Jesus wants us to be holy as his Father is.

• Holiness consists of carrying out God's will with joy.

• Each one of us is what he is in the eyes of God. We are all called to be saints. There is nothing extraordinary about this call. We all have been created in the image of God to love and to be loved.

• The first step to becoming holy is to will it. St. Thomas says, "Sanctity consists in nothing else than a firm resolve, the heroic act of a soul abandoning herself to God. By an upright will we love God, we choose God, we run toward God, we reach him, we possess him." O good, good will which transforms me into the image of God and makes me like him!

• With a will that is whole we love God, we opt for him, we run toward him, we reach him, we possess him. Often, under the pretext of humility, of confidence, of abandonment, we forget about using our will. But it all depends on these words—*I want* or *I do not want.* I have to pour all of my energy into the words *I want.*

• If we earnestly desire holiness, self-denial must enter our lives fully after prayer. The easiest form of self-denial is control over our bodily senses. We must practice interior mortification and bodily penances also. How generous are we with God in our mortifications?

• A day alone with Jesus is apt to spur us on in the vigorous pursuit of holiness through personal love for Jesus. Jesus desires our perfection with unspeakable ardor. "It is God's will that you grown in holiness" (1 Thes 4:3). His Sacred Heart is filled with an insatiable longing to see us advance toward holiness.

• Am I convinced of Christ's love for me and mine for him? This conviction is like a sunlight which makes the sap of life rise and the buds of sanctity bloom. This conviction is the rock on which sanctity is built. What must we do to get this conviction? We must know Jesus, love Jesus, serve Jesus. We know him through prayers, meditations, and spiritual duties. We love him through holy Mass and the sacraments and through that intimate union of love.

• The church of God needs saints today. This imposes a great responsibility on us sisters, to fight against our own ego and love of comfort that leads us to choose a comfortable and insignificant mediocrity. We are called upon to make our lives a rivalry with Christ; we are called upon to be warriors in saris, for the church needs fighters today. Our war cry has to be "Fight—not flight."

• We need a very deep life of prayer to be able to love as he loves each one of us. We must ask Our Lady, "Dear Mother, teach me to love, prepare me." It's not enough just to join a priesthood or a brotherhood or sisterhood. That's not enough. We need to be more and more humble like Mary and holy like Jesus. If only we are humble like Mary, we can be holy like Jesus. That's all: holy like the Lord.

• Be faithful in little things, for in them our strength lies. To the good God nothing is little, because he is so great and we so small. That is why he stoops down and takes the trouble to make those little things for us—to give us a chance to prove our love for him. Because he makes them, they are very great. He cannot make anything small; they are infinite.

• My prayer for all families is that you grow in holiness through this love for each other. Bring Jesus wherever you go. Let them look up and see only Jesus in you. Pray for your children and pray that your daughters and sons will have the courage to say yes to God and to consecrate their lives totally to him. There are many, many families that would be so happy if their children would give their lives to God. So pray for them that they will be able to fulfill the heart's desire.

• The words "I want to be holy" mean: I will divest myself of everything that is not of God; I will divest myself and empty my heart of material things... I will renounce my own will, my inclinations, my whims, my fickleness; and I will become a generous slave girl to God's will.

• "I am the true vine, and my Father is the vinedresser. Every branch of mine that bears no fruit, he takes away, and every branch that does bear fruit he prunes, that it may bear more fruit" (Jn 15:1-2, RSV).

**Q:** *What is the biggest obstacle that you encounter in your work?*
**MT:** Not being holy yet.

• God said to one of our sisters: "I have so many sisters like you—ordinary, good sisters; I can pave the streets with them. I want fervent ones: saints. 'I looked for one to comfort me and I found none.'"

There is so much unhappiness, so much misery everywhere. Our human nature stays with us from beginning to end. We must work hard every day to conquer ourselves. We must learn to be meek and humble of heart. Let us try to give everything to Jesus: every word, every moment. Jesus, use my eyes, my ears, my feet! My resolution must be firm: to become a saint.

• If you are humble, nothing will touch you, neither praise nor disgrace, because you know what you are. If you are blamed, you won't be discouraged; if anyone calls you a saint, you won't put yourself on a pedestal. If you are a saint, thank God; if you are a sinner don't remain one. Christ tells us to aim very high, not to be like Abraham or David or any of the saints, but to be like our heavenly Father.

• I cannot long for a clear perception of my progress along the route, nor long to know precisely where I am on the path of holiness. I ask Jesus to make me a saint. I leave it to him to choose the means that can lead me in that direction.

• Total surrender to God must come in small details as it comes in big details. It's nothing but that single word, "Yes, I accept whatever you give, and I give whatever you take." And this is just a simple way for us to be holy. We must not create difficulties in our own minds. To be holy doesn't mean to do extraordinary things, to understand big things, but it is a simple acceptance, because I have given myself to God, because I belong to him—my total surrender. He could put me here. He could put me there. He can use me. He can not use me. It doesn't matter because I belong so totally to him that he can do just what he wants to do with me.

• To become holy we need humility and prayer. Jesus taught us how to pray, and he also told us to learn from him to be meek and humble of heart. Neither of these can we do unless we know what is silence. Both humility and prayer grow from an ear, mind, and tongue that have lived in silence with God, for in the silence of the heart God speaks.

• I say to all priests: Be holy and teach us to become holy also. Teach us prayers that will purify our hearts and help us grow in our faith. Remind us of the importance of meditation on Jesus, our source of love and service.

You who have consecrated your lives and your hearts must be poor, chaste, and holy, to be able to say, "This is my body" at the consecration, and to give us this Bread of Life by which we live.

I ask you, I beg you to give all your time to others and fully live your priesthood. Wherever obedience may send you, you must become a living presence of Christ.

• If we really want to grow in holiness through obedience let us turn constantly to Our Lady to teach us how to obey, to Jesus who was obedient unto death: he, being God, "went down and was subject to them."

• Your work on behalf of the poor will be better carried out if you know how God wants you to carry it out, but you will have no way of knowing that, other than by obedience. Submit to your superiors, just like ivy. Ivy cannot live if it does not hold fast to something; you will not grow or live in holiness unless you hold fast to obedience.

• "He, being rich, became poor." It is difficult for a proud person to obey. We do not like to bend, to be humble. To be holy we need obedience. The Gospels are full of the humility of Mary. As spotless as she was, as holy as she was, she obeyed. "Humility of the heart of Jesus, fill my heart." Let us, during the day, pray this prayer often. If there has been resentment in our hearts or if we have not accepted humiliation, we will not learn humility. We cannot learn humility from books. Jesus accepted humiliation. Nothingness cannot disobey. In our lives as Missionaries of Charity, obedience is the greatest gift we can give to God. Jesus came to do the will of his Father, and he did it from the very beginning to the very end.

• Foresight is the beginning of holiness. If you learn this art of foreseeing, you will be more and more like Christ, for his heart was sweet and he would always think about others.

• We all know that there is God who loves us, who has made us. We can turn and ask him, "My Father, help me now. I want to be holy, I want to be good, I want to love." Holiness is not a luxury for the few; it is not just for some people. It is meant for you and for me, for all of us. It is a simple duty, because if we learn to love, we learn to be holy.

# TEN

# *Our Father*

All Christians know the Lord's Prayer. It is the prayer Jesus gave his disciples when they came to him with a request: "Lord, teach us to pray."

The basic prayer is found in the Gospel of Matthew (6:9-13). A shorter form is found in the Gospel of Luke (11:2-4). Today, in spite of various attempts to modernize the language, most English-speaking people say the prayer as it is written on the following page, in the melodious words of the seventeenth century.

Some Christians say "debts" and "debtors" while others say "trespasses" and "those who trespass against us." The importance of forgiveness is clear either way.

The doxology, at the end, is not found in the Bible and is technically not a part of the prayer, though it is often added to it. Different Christians say it differently. A version often set to music is as follows: "For thine is the kingdom, and the power, and the glory forever." Other versions end with "forever and ever." The doxology used here, from the Catholic liturgy, is the one most familiar to Mother Teresa.

All forms of the Lord's Prayer, of course, have the same meaning. It is the one prayer that unites Christians the world around and focuses their hearts on their loving heavenly Father whose kingdom is based on forgiveness of sin, provision of bread, and deliverance from evil.

*Our Father, who art in heaven,*
*hallowed be thy name;*
*thy kingdom come;*
*thy will be done on earth as it is in heaven.*
*Give us this day our daily bread;*
*and forgive us our trespasses*
*as we forgive those who trespass against us;*
*and lead us not into temptation,*
*but deliver us from evil.*

*For the kingdom, the power, and the glory are yours, now and forever. Amen.*

*Our Father, who art in heaven,*
*hallowed be thy name...*

• The apostles asked Jesus to teach them to pray, and he taught them the beautiful prayer, the "Our Father." I believe each time we say the "Our Father," God looks at his hands, where he has carved us—"I have carved you on the palm of my hand"—he looks at his hands, and he sees us there. How wonderful the tenderness and love of the great God!

• Prayer, to be fruitful, must come from the heart and must be able to touch the heart of God. See how Jesus taught his disciples to pray. Call God your Father; praise and glorify his name. Do his will as the saints do it in heaven; ask for daily bread, spiritual and temporal; ask for forgiveness of your own sins and that you may forgive others, and also for the grace not to give in to temptations and for the final grace to be delivered from the evil that is in us and around us.

• Where can I learn to pray? Jesus taught us: "Pray like this: Our Father... thy will be done... forgive us as we forgive." It is so simple yet so beautiful. If we pray the "Our Father," and live it, we will be holy. Everything is there: God, myself, my neighbor. If I forgive, then I can be holy and can pray. All this comes from a humble heart, and if we have this we will know how to love God, to love self, and to love our neighbor.

This is not complicated, and yet we complicate our lives so much, by so many additions. Just one thing counts: to be humble, to pray. The more you pray, the better you will pray.

How do you pray? You should go to God like a little child. A child has no difficulty expressing his little mind in simple words which say so much. Jesus said to Nicodemus: "Become as a little child." If we pray the gospel, we will allow Christ to grow in us.

• Christ's teaching is so simple that even a very young child can babble it. The apostles asked, "Teach us to pray." Jesus answered, "When you pray, say 'Our Father...'" (see Luke 11:1-4).

• We must be aware of our oneness with Christ, as he was aware of oneness with his Father. Our work is truly apostolic only in so far as we permit him to work in us and through us, with his power, with his desire, and with his love.

• St. Clement related having heard from St. Peter that our Lord was accustomed to watch like a mother with her children, near his disciples during their sleep to render them any little service.

• Total surrender involves loving trust. You cannot surrender totally unless you trust lovingly and totally. Jesus trusted his Father because he knew him, he knew of his love. "My Father and I are one." "The Father is in me and I am in the Father." "I am not alone, the Father is with me." "Father, into your hands I commend my Spirit." Read St. John's Gospel and see how many times Jesus used the word "Father." Jesus came to reveal the Father. In the time of the Old Testament God was known as the God of fear, punishment, and anger. The coming of Jesus reverses this picture completely. God in the New Testament is the God of love, compassion, and mercy. That is why we can trust him fully—there is no more fear. This loving trust implies that we know the love of God and that we proclaim this love, compassion, and mercy everywhere we are sent. Today we reveal him.

• Loving trust means for our contemplative life—
 —an absolute, unconditional, and unwavering confidence in God our loving Father, even when everything seems to be a total failure;
 —to look to him alone as our help and protector;
 —to stop doubting and being discouraged, casting all our worries and cares on the Lord, and walking in total freedom;
 —to be daring and absolutely fearless of any obstacle, knowing that nothing is impossible with God;
 —total reliance on our Heavenly Father with a spontaneous abandonment of the little children, totally convinced of our utter nothingness but trusting to the point of rashness with courageous confidence in his fatherly goodness.

• Every Missionary of Charity will pray with absolute trust in God's loving care for us. Our prayer will be the prayer of little children, one of tender devotion, deep reverence, humility, serenity, and simplicity.

*... thy kingdom come...*

• We put our hands, our eyes, and our hearts at Christ's disposal, so that he will act through us.

• Our particular mission is to labor at the salvation and sanctification of the poorest of the poor not only in the slums but all over the world, wherever they may be, by—
 —living the love of God in prayer and action in a life marked by the simplicity and humility of the gospel;
 —loving Jesus under the appearance of bread;
 —serving him in the distressing disguise of the poorest of the poor, both materially and spiritually, recognizing in them and restoring to them the image and likeness of God.

As members of the active branch by—
— nursing the sick and the dying destitutes;
— gathering and teaching little street children;
— visiting and caring for beggars, leprosy patients, and their children;
— giving shelter to the abandoned and homeless;
— caring for the unwanted, the unloved, and the lonely;
— going out to the spiritually poorest of the poor to proclaim the Word of God by our presence and spiritual works of mercy;
— adoration of Jesus in the Blessed Sacrament.

• We cannot take charge of works that would divert us from the slums, from the neighborhoods of misery. That is the kingdom of Christ and ours—our working field. If a son abandons the field of his father and goes to work in another field, he ceases to be a co-worker of his father. Those who share everything are partners who give love for love, suffering for suffering. Jesus has given us everything—his life, his blood, everything. Now it is our turn. We cannot desert his field.

• If we really want to conquer the world, we will not be able to do it with bombs or with other weapons of destruction. Let us conquer the world with our love. Let us interweave our lives with bonds of sacrifice and love, and it will be possible for us to conquer the world.

• In the slums the sisters should find a place where they will gather little street children, whoever they may be. Their very first concern is to make them clean, feed them and only then teach them, and prepare them for admission into regular schools. The love of God must be proposed to them in a simple, interesting, and attractive way.

The sisters shall visit the destitute and the sick, going from house to house or wherever these may be found, and they must render to all the humblest services. They shall also visit the jails.

• We shall—
— call sinners to repentance;

— instruct the ignorant;
— counsel the doubtful;
— sustain the tempted;
— befriend the friendless and comfort the sick and sorrowful;
— bear wrongs patiently: trusting in God for deliverance in his own good time;
— forgive injuries;
— bring prayer into the lives of the spiritually poorest of the poor.

• It is you, sisters, who can fill the world with the love that God has given you. The work of moral rearmament is carried out with discretion and love. The more discrete, the more penetrating it will be. You give it to others, and it is they who absorb it.

• Is it not our mission to give God to the poor of the street? Not a dead God but a living God, a God of love.

• What is the Good News? The Good News is that God still loves the world through each one of you. You are God's Good News, you are God's love in action. Through you, God is still loving the world.

• We ought every day to renew our resolution and to rouse ourselves to fervor, as if it were the first day of our conversion, saying, "Help me, Lord God, in my good resolve and in thy holy service, and give me grace this very day really and truly to begin, for what I have done till now is nothing." This is the spirit in which we should begin our monthy recollection day.

• We shall make this year one of peace in a particular way. To be able to do this we shall try to talk more to God and with God and less with men and to men. Let us preach the peace of Christ as he did. He went about doing good; he did not stop his works of charity because the Pharisees and others hated him or tried to spoil his Father's work. He just went about doing good.

• Our lives, to be fruitful, must be full of Christ; to be able to bring his peace, joy, and love we must have it ourselves, for we cannot give what we have not got—the blind leading the blind. The poor in the slums are without Jesus and we have the privilege of entering their homes. What they think of us does not matter, but what we are to them does matter. To go to the slums merely for the sake of going will not be enough to draw them to Jesus. If you are preoccupied with yourself and your own affairs, you will not be able to live up to this ideal.

• Zeal for souls is the effect and the proof of true love of God. We cannot but be consumed with the desire for saving souls, the greatest and dearest interest of Jesus. Therefore, zeal is the test of love and the test of zeal is devotedness to his cause—spending life and energy in the work of souls.

• In the Spirit, both of our congregations are carriers of God's love. We the sisters carry God's love in action, you brothers of the Word carry God's love in evangelization, but we are all carriers, we all are missionaries. The mission of proclaiming Christ, through action or through words, is one mission, the mission of love and compassion. For the sake of making things simpler we have different names, but this is just for external reasons. Actually it is the same thing: we all work for the proclamation of God's kingdom.

• We all long for heaven where God is, but we have it in our power to be in heaven with him right now, to be happy with him this moment. But being happy with him now means loving as he loves, helping as he helps, giving as he gives, serving as he serves, rescuing as he rescues—and being with him twenty-four hours a day.

• An Indian physician, as he saw the care a sister devoted to a sick man who had been declared hopeless by his colleagues, said, "I came here without God. I'm now going back with God."

• The sisters do small things—helping children, visiting those who are isolated, the sick, those who lack everything.

In one of the houses the sisters visit they found a woman who had died alone a few days earlier. Her body had already begun decomposing. The neighbors didn't even know her name.

When someone tells me that what the sisters do is irrelevant, that they limit themselves to things that are little less than ordinary, I reply that even if they helped only one person, that would be reason enough for their work. Jesus would have died for one person, for one sinner.

*... thy will be done on earth as it is in heaven.*

• Today, more than ever, we need to pray for the light to know the will of God, for the love to accept the will of God, for the way to do the will of God.

• It is not possible to engage in the direct apostolate without being a soul of prayer, without a conscious awareness and submission to the divine will.

• In his passion our Lord says, "Thy will be done. Do with me what you want." And that was the hardest thing for our Lord even at the last moment. They say that the passion in Gethsemane was much greater than even the crucifixion. Because it was his heart, his soul that was being crucified, while on the cross it was his body that was crucified. That's why on the cross he never said, "Thy will be done." He accepted in silence, and he gave his mother, and he said, "I thirst" and "It is finished." But not once did he say "Thy will be done," because he had already totally accepted during that terrible struggle of the isolation and the loneliness. And the only way that we know that it was so difficult for him that hour is that he asked, "Why could you not spend one hour with me?"—we know he needed consolation. This is total surrender: not to be loved by anybody, not to be wanted by anybody, just to be a nobody because we have given all to Christ.

• "I will be a saint" means I will despoil myself of all that is not God. I will strip my heart and empty it of all created things; I will live in poverty and detachment. I will renounce my will, my inclinations, my whims and fancies, and make myself a willing slave to the will of God. Yes, my children, this is what I pray for daily—for each one—that we each may become a slave to the will of God.

• We must become holy not because we want to feel holy, but because Christ must be able to live his life fully in us. We are to be all love, all faith, all purity for the sake of the poor we serve. Once we have learned to seek first God and his will, our contacts with the poor will become the means of great sanctity to ourselves and to others. Holiness is union with God; so in prayer and action alike we come from God in Christ and go to God through Christ.

• The perfect will of God for us: you must be holy. Holiness is the greatest gift that God can give us because for that reason he created us.

• Jesus is going to do great things with you if you let him do it and if you don't try to interfere with him. We interfere with God's plans when we push in someone or something else not suitable for us. Be very strict with yourself, and then be very strict with what you are receiving from outside. People may come with wonderful ideas, with beautiful things, but anything that takes you away from the reality of what you have given to God must remain outside.

• The suffering of the Church is caused by a misunderstanding of freedom and renewal. We cannot be free unless we are able to renounce our own will for Christ's. We cannot be renewed without the humility to recognize what needs to be renewed in ourselves. Distrust those who come to you with dazzling words about freedom and renewal: they are deceivers.

• This doing of the will of God is obedience. Jesus came to do the will of his Father and did it unto death, death on the cross. "Be it done to me according to your word," was Our Lady's answer for you and for me when we have been chosen to be his own by becoming Missionaries of Charity. The surest way to true holiness and the fulfillment of our mission of peace, love, and joy is through obedience.

• We must have a real, living resolution to reach holiness. St. Teresa says that Satan is terribly afraid of resolute souls. Everything depends on these two or three words: "I will" or "I will not." I must put all my energy into this "will." St. John Berchmans, St. Stanislaus, and St. Margaret Mary said "I will," and they did become saints.

What is a saint but simply a resolute soul, a soul that uses power plus action? Wasn't this what St. Paul meant when he said: "I can do all things in him who strengthens me?" My sisters, I will not be satisfied if you are just good religious. I want to be able to offer God a perfect sacrifice. Only holiness perfects the gift.

*Give us this day our daily bread...*

• Our lives have to be more and more penetrated by a deep faith in Jesus, the Bread of Life, which must be eaten with and for the poor.

• Where will you get the joy of loving?—in the Eucharist, Holy Communion. Jesus has made himself the Bread of Life to give us life. Night and day, he is there.

• To make it easy for you and for me to see Jesus, he made himself the Bread of Life, so that we can receive life, so that we may have a life of peace, a life of joy. Find Jesus, and you will find peace.

• People are hungry for God. People are hungry for love. Are you aware of that? Do you know that? Do you see that? Do you have eyes to see? Quite often we look but we don't see. We are all passing through this world. We need to open our eyes and see.

• When I pick up a hungry person from the streets, I give him a plate of rice, a piece of bread, and I have satisfied that hunger; but a person that is shut out, that feels unwanted, unloved, terrified, the person that has been thrown out of society—how much more difficult it is to remove that hunger.

• A few weeks ago, I picked up a child from the street, and from the face I could see that little child was hungry. I didn't know how many days that little one had not eaten. So I gave her a piece of bread, and the little one took the bread and, crumb by crumb, started eating it. I said to her, "Eat, eat the bread. You are hungry." And the little one looked at me and said, "I am afraid. When the bread will be finished, I will be hungry again."

• We cook for nine thousand people every day. One day one sister came and said, "Mother, there's nothing to eat, nothing to give to the people." I had no answer. And then by nine o'clock that morning a truck full of bread came to our house. The government gives a slice of bread and milk each day to the poor children. That day—no one in the city knew why—but suddenly all the schools were closed. And all the bread came to Mother Teresa. See, God closed the schools. He would not let our people go without food. And this was the first time, I think, in their lives that they had had such good bread and so much. This way you can see the tenderness of God.

• When communicating with Christ in your heart after partaking of the Living Bread, remember what Our Lady must have felt when the Holy Spirit overpowered her, and she who was full of grace became full with the body of Christ. The spirit in her was so strong that immediately she "rose in haste" to go and serve.

• Jesus has made himself the Bread of Life to satisfy my hunger for him, and he has also made himself the hungry one so that I may satisfy his love for me. He is hungry for us just as we are hungry for him. Universal Brothers of the Word, find out that the Word has to become flesh first in your life, coming among you in love, in unity, in peace, in joy, and then you will be able to give it to the spiritually poorest, to give it to that man sitting in the park, drunk and all by himself.

• The world today is hungry not only for bread but hungry for love; hungry to be wanted, to be loved. They're hungry to feel that presence of Christ. In many countries, people have everything except that presence, that understanding. That's why the life of prayer and sacrifice comes to give that love. By being contemplative, you are to be that presence, that bread of God to break.

• Let us now pray thus:
Lord, make us worthy to serve our brothers,
men of all the world,
who live and die in poverty and hunger.
Give them this day, through our hands, their daily bread.
And through our love and understanding, give them peace
and joy. Amen.

• Even if this year we should collect less money, much less, the important thing is that we continue to spread Christ's love. If we give Christ to him who is hungry—not only for bread but also for our love, for our presence, for our contact—then this year could well be the year of the real live explosion of the love that God brings to our earth.

• Jesus gives me the opportunity to feed him by feeding those who are hungry, to clothe him by clothing those who are naked, to heal him by caring for those who are sick, and to offer him shelter by housing those who are homeless and unwanted.

• To be able to do something beautiful for God, we need Jesus. Jesus became the Bread of Life so that you and I, and even a small child, can receive him and have life. In a special way we need the Bread of Life to know the poor, to love them, and serve them. Each one of us needs to encounter Jesus. Without him, we can do nothing. We need the Bread of Life to live. Jesus said very clearly, "If you do not eat my flesh and drink my blood, you will not have eternal life."

• The Gospels remind us that Jesus, before he taught the people, felt compassion for the multitudes that followed after him. Sometimes he felt it even to the point of forgetting to eat. How did he put his compassion into practice? He multiplied the loaves of bread and the fish to satisfy their hunger. He gave them food to eat until they couldn't eat any more, and twelve basketsful were left over. Then he taught them. Only then did he tell them the Good News. This is what we must often do in our work: we must first satisfy the needs of the body, so we can then bring Christ to the poor.

• When Jesus came into the world, he loved it so much that he gave his life for it. He wanted to satisfy our hunger for God. And what did he do? He made himself the Bread of Life. He became small, fragile, and defenseless for us. Bits of bread can be so small that even a baby can chew it, even a dying person can eat it. He became the Bread of Life to satisfy our hunger for God, our hunger for love.

• Jesus, being rich, became poor for you and for me. I don't think we could have ever loved God if Jesus had never become one of us. So that we might be able to love God, he himself became one of us in all things, except sin.

It was not enough for him to become poor like us. He made himself the Bread of Life. And he said, "Unless you eat my flesh and drink my blood, you cannot live, you cannot have eternal life" (see John 6:53-54).

If we have been created in the image of God, then we have been created to love, because God is love. We have been created for great things.

• By daily feeding on the Scriptures, particularly the New Testament, we shall grow in a deeper and more personal knowledge and love of Jesus Christ and his teachings, so as to be able to feed his children with his divine Word. We shall be painstaking and diligent in studying and memorizing selected passages, daily reading and meditating on the Scriptures—to be able to know and love God personally.

• Lord, make us worthy to serve men, our brothers, who are dispersed all over the world, who live and die in poverty and hunger. Give to all of them, through our hands, their daily bread, and through our understanding love give them peace and joy.

• We have to feed ourselves. We can die from spiritual starvation.

*... and forgive us our trespasses...*

• It is much easier to conquer a country than to conquer ourselves. Every act of disobedience weakens my spiritual life. It is like a wound letting out every drop of one's blood. Nothing can cause this havoc in our spiritual life as quickly as disobedience.

• Just as the rigorous winter prepares the way for spring, penance prepares us for the sanctity of God, filling us with his vision and love. It makes us more and more sinless and attunes us to the work of the Spirit within us, bringing our whole being under the powerful influence of Jesus. It plunges us into the deep contemplation of God.

• One thing is necessary for us—confession. Confession is nothing but humility in action. We used to call it penance, but really it is a sacrament of love, a sacrament of forgiveness. That is why confession should not be a place in which to talk for long hours about our difficulties. It is a place where I allow Jesus to take away from me everything that divides, that destroys. When there is a gap between me and Christ, when my love is divided, anything can come to fill the gap. We should be very simple and childlike in confession. "Here I am as a child going to her Father." If a child is not yet spoiled and has not learned to tell lies, he will tell everything. This is what I mean by being childlike. Confession is a beautiful act of great love. Only in confession can we go as sinners with sin and come out as sinners without sin.

• Confession makes the soul strong because a really good confession—the confession of a child in sin coming back to her Father—always begets humility, and humility is strength. We may go to confession as often as we want and to whom we want, but we are not encouraged to seek spiritual direction from any and every source. The confessional is not a place for useless conversation or gossip. The topic should be my sins, my sorrow, my forgiveness: how to overcome my temptations, how to practice virtue, how to increase in the love of God.

• First, confession; after it ask for spiritual direction if necessary. The reality of my sins must come first. For most of us there is the danger of forgetting that we are sinners and must go to confession as sinners. We must want the Precious Blood to wash away our sins. We must go to God to tell him we are sorry for all we have done which may have hurt him.

• We come from confession a sinner without sin by the greatness of the mercy of God. No need for us to despair. No need for us to commit suicide. No need for us to be discouraged—no need, if we have understood the tenderness of God's love. You are precious to him. He loves you, and he loves you so tenderly that he has carved you on the palm of his hand. These are God's words written in the Scripture. You know that. Remember that when your heart feels restless, when your heart feels hurt, when your heart feels like breaking—then remember, "I am precious to him. He loves me. He has called me by my name. I am his. He loves me. God loves me." And to prove that love he died on the cross.

• During Lent we shall in a special way and with deep feeling meditate on the passion of our Lord and examine our conscience on what sin of ours caused that special pain to Jesus. I will make reparation and share that pain by doubling my penance. I shall keep strict custody of my eyes; I shall keep clean thoughts in my mind; I shall touch the sick with greater gentleness and compassion; I shall keep the silence of the heart with greater care, so that in the silence of my heart I hear his words of comfort and from the fullness of my heart I comfort Jesus in the distressing disguise of the poor. I shall confess especially my neglect of penance.

• Penance is absolutely necessary for us. Nothing is of greater force in restraining the disordered passions of the soul and in subjecting the natural appetites to right reason. Then we shall possess those heavenly joys and delights that surpass the pleasure of earth as much as the soul does the body, and heaven the earth.

• Let us often say during the day, "Wash away my sins and cleanse me from all my iniquity." How it must hurt Jesus dwelling in our heart to feel in our hearts this bitterness, this hurt, this revengeful feeling made of jealousy and pride! My children, let us be sincere and ask to be forgiven.

• We shall spend two hours a day at sunrise and sunset in adoration of Jesus in the Blessed Sacrament exposed. Our hours of adoration will be special hours of reparation for sins and intercession for the needs of the whole world, exposing the sin-sick and suffering humanity to the healing, sustaining, and transforming rays of Jesus, radiating from the Eucharist.

• Our penance is an act of perfect love of God, man, and the whole universe. It seeks to reconcile man with God, man with man, and man with God's creation, bringing about the unity in Jesus, with Jesus, and through Jesus of all that was disrupted by sin. It is for us a joyful identification with Christ crucified; it is a hunger to be lost in him, so that nothing remains of us but he alone in his radiant glory drawing all men to the Father. "Unless the grain of wheat falls to the earth and dies, it remains just a grain of wheat. But if it dies, it produces much fruit" (Jn 12:24).

• The other day, a man, a journalist, asked me a strange question. He asked me, "Even you, do you have to go to confession?"

I said, "Yes, I go to confession every week."

And he said, "Then God must be very demanding if you all have to go to confession."

And I said, "Your own child sometimes does something wrong. What happens when your child comes to you and says, 'Daddy, I'm sorry'? What do you do? You put both of your arms around your child and kiss him. Why? Because that's your way of telling him that you love him. God does the same thing. He loves you tenderly."

Even when we sin or make a mistake, let's allow that to help us grow closer to God. Let's tell him humbly, "I know I shouldn't have done this, but even this failure I offer to you."

• If we have sinned or made a mistake, let us go to him and say, "I'm sorry! I repent." God is a forgiving Father. His mercy is greater than our sins. He will forgive us. This is humility: to have the courage to accept such humiliation and receive God's forgiveness.

*... as we forgive those who trespass against us...*

• Is my love for the other members of the community so great, so real as to forgive, not out of duty but out of love?

• We often pray, "Let me share with you your pain; I want to be the spouse of Jesus crucified," and yet when a little spittle of an uncharitable remark or a thorn of thoughtlessness is given to us, how we forget that this is the time to share with him his shame and pain.

• One day I found among the debris a woman who was burning with fever. About to die, she kept repeating, "It is my son who has done it!" I took her in my arms and carried her home to the convent. On the way I urged her to forgive her son. It took a good while before I could hear her say, "Yes, I forgive him." She said it with a feeling of genuine forgiveness, just as she was about to pass away.

The woman was not aware that she was dying, that she was burning with fever, that she was suffering. What was breaking her heart was her own son's lack of love.

• In his passion Jesus taught us how to forgive out of love, how to forget out of humility. So let us at the beginning of the passion of Christ examine our hearts fully and see if there is any unforgiven hurt or unforgotten bitterness.

**Q:** *Is it necessary to be a Christian in order to forgive?*
**MT:** No, it is not absolutely necessary. Every human being comes from the hand of God, and we all know something of God's love for us. Whatever our religion, we know that if we really want to love, we must learn to forgive before anything else.

• Let us think about oppressed countries. The greatest need of Bangladesh is forgiveness—there is so much bitterness and hatred! It is impossible to imagine how those people suffer. If they realize that we care for them, that we love them, perhaps they will find strength in their hearts to forgive. I think this is the only thing that can bring them peace.

• Reconciliation begins with ourselves. It begins with a pure heart, a heart that is able to see God in others.

• The tongue, that part of the body that makes such direct contact with the body of Christ, can become an instrument of joy or of suffering. Do not go to bed when you know that your sister has something against you.

• Some young people who ran away from home have gotten sick with AIDS. We have opened a home in New York for AIDS patients, who find themselves among the most unwanted people of today.

What a tremendous change has been brought about in their lives just because of a few sisters who take care of them, and have made a home for them!

A home of love!
A gift of love!

A place, perhaps the only place, where they feel loved, where they are somebody to someone. This has changed their lives in such a way that they die a most beautiful death. Not one of them has yet died in distress.

The other day, a sister called to tell me that one of the young men (all are young people) was dying. But, strange to say, he couldn't die.

So she asked him, "What is it?" (He was struggling with death!) "What is wrong?"

And he said, "Sister, I cannot die until I ask my father to forgive me."

So the sister found out where the father was, and she called him. And something extraordinary happened, like a living page from the Gospel: The father embraced his son and cried, "My son! My beloved son!"

And the son begged the father, "Forgive me! Forgive me!"

And the two of them clung to each other tenderly.

Two hours later the young man died.

• Christians need to learn to forgive. We have to be forgiven in order to be able to forgive. I believe that if the people in Belfast—just like elsewhere in Bangladesh, Amman, New York, and other places—would forgive each other, world peace would come.

**Q:** *How does one learn to forgive?*
**MT:** By knowing that we too need to be forgiven.
**Q:** *Could you verify the need for forgiveness in Belfast?*
**MT:** I have seen this in several families that I have visited where someone was murdered or someone died violently. There is no prejudice in these families. I have seen that these families have forgiven and don't hold any grudges against the ones who killed their sons. I think that is a first step.

• When we realize that we are sinners needing forgiveness, it will be very easy for us to forgive others. If I do not understand this, it will be very hard for me to say "I forgive you" to anyone who comes to me.

*... and lead us not into temptation,*
*but deliver us from evil.*

• Let us ask our Lord to be with us in our moments of temptation. Just as Jesus was tempted, the devil will also tempt us. We must not be afraid, because God loves us and will not fail to help us.

• We must be convinced that nothing adorns a human soul with greater splendor than the virtue of chastity and nothing defiles a human soul more than the opposite vice. Yet there must be no mistake that the glory of chastity is not in immunity from temptation but in victory over these temptations.

• When we recollect that in the morning we have held within our hands an all-holy God, we are more ready to abstain from whatever could soil their purity. Hence deep reverence for our own person; reverence for others, treating all with accepted marks of courtesy, but abstaining from sentimental feelings or ill-ordered affections.

• If we love God with our whole soul, if we have a love of Jesus Christ above all things, if we have a tender love for Our Lady, we shall be less inclined to be unduly attached to creatures. In order that the love for Jesus may produce these effects, it must be intense, generous, and all-absorbing. It will so fill the mind and heart that we no longer give a thought to human affections. Should we unfortunately become entangled in any ill-ordered affections, Jesus who cannot suffer strange gods in our hearts will reproach us severely. He will himself protect with jealous care the hearts of those who give themselves to him.

• By yourselves you can get nothing but weakness, misery, and sin. All the gifts you have come from God. Do not allow temptations to weaken the strength of your vocation.

• Self-knowledge puts us on our knees, and it is very necessary for love. For knowledge of God produces love, and knowledge of self produces humility. Self-knowledge is a very important thing in our lives. As St. Augustine says, "Fill yourselves first, and then only will you be able to give to others." Self-knowledge is also a safeguard against pride, especially when one is tempted later in life. The greatest mistake is to think one is too strong to fall into temptation. Put your finger in the fire and it will burn. Don't play with temptation.

• In my heart there is only one vacant seat. It is for God and nobody else. Temptation is like fire in which gold is purified. So we have to go through this fire. The temptations are allowed by God. The only thing we have to do is to refuse to give in. If I say I do not want it, I am safe. There may be temptations against purity, against faith, against my vocation. If we love our vocation, we will be tempted. But then we will also grow in sanctity. We have to fight temptation for the love of God.

• Don't allow anything to interfere with your love for Jesus. You belong to him. Nothing can separate you from him. That one sentence is important to remember. He will be your joy, your strength. If you hold onto that sentence, temptations and difficulties will come, but nothing will break you.

• If we really want to know whether something is a temptation, let us examine our obedience. It is the best light in time of temptation, and we will know exactly where we are and what we are doing. It is the best light in that terrible darkness. Even for Jesus, the devil wanted to find out who he was. He was not sure. The devil will stoop to anything to find out where our weak point is. He will do anything to get us to accept that one wrong thought, to say that one unkind word, to do that one impure act, that one act of disobedience, that one instance of giving something away without permission, that one neglect of prayer—just that one thing. If there is an award to be given for patience it should be given to the devil. He has a lot of patience.

• Joy is one of the best safeguards against temptation. The devil is a carrier of dust and dirt; he uses every chance to throw what he has at us. A joyful heart knows how to protect herself from such dirt. Jesus can take full possession of our soul only if it surrenders itself joyfully. "A saint who is sad is a sad saint," St. Francis de Sales used to say. St. Thérèse was worried about her sisters only when she saw any of them lose their joy.

• Don't be afraid. There must be the cross, there must be suffering—a clear sign that Jesus has drawn you so close to his heart that he can share his suffering with you.

• Without God we can spread only pain and suffering around us.

• The Lord has willed me here where I am. He will offer a solution.

• One cannot hide the fact that active life is full of risks because of the numerous opportunities that it offers for sin. But we can be confident of God's special protection in every action we carry out under the sign of obedience. Doubting when obedience calls you to action is something that deserves the reproach of Jesus to Peter: "How little faith you have!... Why did you falter?" (Mt 14:31).

• "Blessed are those who suffer persecution": We do not suffer much persecution, except the persecution caused by the devil against chastity, poverty, obedience, and wholehearted free service. To resist this persecution we need continual refilling of prayer and sacrifice—of the Bread of Life, of the Living Water, of my sisters in community, and of the poor. We need Our Lady, our mother, to be with us always, to protect us and keep us only for Jesus.

• Suffering will never be completely absent from our lives. Through it, we are given the chance to share the joy of loving Jesus in his passion—it is beautiful to think of that! So don't be afraid of suffering. Your suffering, too, is a great means of love, if you make use of it, especially if you offer it for peace in the world.

*... For the kingdom, the power, and the glory*
*are yours, now and for ever.*

• "I kept the Lord ever before my eyes, because he is ever at my right hand, that I may not slip" (see Psalm 25:15), says the psalmist. God is within me with a more intimate presence than that whereby I am in myself: "In him we live and move and have our being" (Acts 17:28). It is he who gives life to all, who gives power and being to all that exists. But for his sustaining presence, all things would cease to be and fall back into nothingness. Consider that you are in God, surrounded and encompassed by God, swimming in God.

• With God, nothing is impossible. Our sisters are living proof of that. When I watch them, I receive the infinite greatness of God, a greatness that we can tap into. I see how he can work through us. Because you and I have nothing on our own, we need him. As the Bible says, God waits and looks. Will we respond?

Just consider what God has accomplished through the sisters and the Co-workers scattered throughout the world. We must ponder it in order to admire the greatness of God shown among us. This is not pride. It takes humility to recognize the greatness of God shining through us. Boasting of our greatness before men is pride. Great humility arises when we recognize that it is God's kindness and his greatness that shows through our hands, our work, and our love because that is the simple truth.

Jesus is the truth that must be shared. All those who have witnessed our work, have been able to see that God is the source. Just as Jesus said, "Likewise, when men see your good deeds, they will give praise to your Father who is in heaven" (see Matthew 5:16).

• Pray for us, that we do not spoil the work of God, that this may always be the work of God. Pray for our poor, the old, the unwanted children, the sick, the lepers, for those who suffer from AIDS, for all those we can serve as a gift from God. Let us ask our Lord to grant us the grace to serve our brothers and sisters throughout the world who live and die in poverty and misery.

*Lord, give them, today, through our hands, their daily bread! Grant that, through our understanding love, we may bring them peace and joy. Let us never forget that what we do with love always brings peace.*

# ELEVEN

## *This Is the Lamb of God*

When the priest invites the worshipers to come forward to receive the Bread of Life, he says the words of John the Baptist, the prophet who prepared the way for Jesus: "Behold, the Lamb of God, who takes away the sin of the world!" (Jn 1:29, RSV). The people who heard John the Baptist knew that a lamb was an animal used as a sacrifice. The Eucharist is a thanksgiving for Christ's sacrifice on the cross so that the world might be saved.

The priest also says words recorded in the Book of Revelation (see 19:9): "Blessed are those who have been called to the wedding feast of the Lamb." The sacrificed Lamb is risen from the dead and reigns with God in heaven. The priest invites those who love Jesus to join in the celebration.

Before entering into communion with Christ in the Eucharist, the worshipers acknowledge that it is God's grace and not their own worth that allows them to come to him. The words "Lord, I am not worthy..." come from a beautiful story found in the Gospel of Luke (7:6-7). A Roman army officer used similar words to beg Jesus to heal a dying slave. Jesus healed the slave and praised the officer for his faith. The same way, Jesus responds to everyone who comes to him and asks to be made whole. This is a wonderful reason for Eucharist, for thanksgiving!

Priest: *This is the Lamb of God who takes away the sins of the world. Happy are those who are called to his supper.*

People: *Lord, I am not worthy to receive you, but only say the word and I shall be healed.*

*This is the Lamb of God*
*who takes away the sins of the world.*
*Happy are those who are called to his supper.*

• The Eucharist is the sacrament of prayer, the fountain and summit of Christian life. Our Eucharist is incomplete if it does not lead us to service and love for the poor. As we receive the communion of the poor, we discover our own poverty.

• Our life is linked to the Eucharist. Through faith in and love of the body of Christ under the appearance of bread, we take Christ literally: "I was hungry and you gave me food. I was a stranger and you welcomed me, naked and you clothed me."

• Put your sins in the chalice for the Precious Blood to wash away. One drop is capable of washing away all the sins of the world.

• We need the Eucharist because Jesus has become the Bread of Life in order to meet our desires, our longings, our love for him. This is why our life needs to be closely linked to the Eucharist. We begin our day with the holy Mass and Communion, and we finish the day with an hour of adoration, which unites us with Jesus and with the poor in whom we offer our services.

• Let us stop for a moment to think about the tenderness of God's love for us. There are thousands of people who would love to have what you have. And yet God has chosen you to be where you are today to share the joy of loving others.

To make this love more real, more loving, more living, he gives himself as the Bread of Life. He gives us his own life. He wants us to love one another, to give ourselves to each other until it hurts. It does not matter how much we give, but how much love we put into our giving.

In the Constitution of the Missionaries of Charity, we have a beautiful part which speaks of the tenderness of Christ, and also of his faithful friendship and love. To make that love more living, more sure, more tender, Jesus gives us the Eucharist. This is why it is necessary for every Missionary of Charity to feed upon the Eucharist in order to be a true carrier of God's love. She must live on the Eucharist and have her heart and life woven with the Eucharist. No Missionary of Charity can give Jesus if she does not have Jesus in her heart.

• Someone could ask, "Who are the poorest of the poor?" They are the unwanted, the unloved, the uncared for, the hungry, the forgotten, the naked, the homeless, the lepers, the alcoholics. But also we Missionaries of Charity are the poorest of the poor.

To be able to do what we do, and live the kind of life we live, every Missionary of Charity has to have her life united with the Eucharist. In the Eucharist, we see Christ in the appearance of bread. Then in the poor, we see Christ in a distressing disguise. The Eucharist and the poor are but one love.

To be able to work, to be able to see, to be able to love, we need this eucharistic union.

• As Missionaries of Charity we are especially called upon to see Christ in the appearance of bread and to touch him in the broken bodies of the poor.

When he took bread, Christ said: "Take and eat, this is my body delivered for you." By giving himself, he invites us to grow in the power of his love to do what he has done.

Christ's love for us will give us strength and urge us to spend ourselves for him. "Let the sisters and the people eat you up." We have no right to refuse our life to others in whom we contact Christ.

• We cannot separate our lives from the Eucharist; the moment we do, something breaks. People ask, "Where do the sisters get the joy and energy to do what they are doing?"

The Eucharist involves more than just receiving; it also involves satisfying the hunger of Christ. He says, "Come to me." He is hungry for souls. Nowhere does the Gospel say: "Go away," but always "Come to me."

Our lives must be woven around the Eucharist. Ask Jesus to be with you, to work with you that you may be able to pray the work. You must really be sure that you have received Jesus. After that, you cannot give your tongue, your thoughts, or your heart to bitterness.

• The Eucharist is connected with the passion. If Jesus had not established the Eucharist we would have forgotten the crucifixion. It would have faded into the past and we would have forgotten that Jesus loved us.

There is a saying that to be far away from the eyes is to be far away from the heart. To make sure that we do not forget, Jesus gave us the Eucharist as a memorial of his love. To make sure that we keep on loving him, he gives us his hunger (to satisfy our hunger for him)—he gives us the poorest of the poor.

We must be faithful to that smallness of the Eucharist, that simple piece of bread which even a child can take in, that giving of a bath, that smile. We have so much that we don't care about the small things. If we do not care, we will lose our grip on the Eucharist—on our lives. The Eucharist is so small.

I was giving Communion this morning. My two fingers were holding Jesus. Try to realize that Jesus allows himself to be broken. Make yourselves feel the need of each other. The passion and the Eucharist should open our eyes to that smallness: "This is my body; take and eat"—the small piece of bread. Today let us realize our own littleness in comparison with the Bread of Life.

• For us, we must never separate the Eucharist and the poor—or the poor and the Eucharist. You will really be a true Missionary of Charity when you go to the poor and take Jesus with you. He satisfied my hunger for him and now I go to satisfy his hunger for souls, for love.

That is why Jesus made himself bread, to satisfy our hunger for God. See the humility of God. He also made himself the hungry one to satisfy our hunger for God through our love, our service. Let us pray that none of us will be unfaithful. Let us pray for our poor people. They are also hungry for God.

• God so loved the world that he gave his Son. He gave him to Mary, that she would be his mother. Jesus became a person, just like you and me, except without sin. And he showed his love to us by giving us his life, his whole being.

He made himself poor though he was rich—for you and for me. He gave himself up completely. He died on the cross. But before dying he became the Bread of Life—in order to meet our hunger for love.

He said, "If you do not eat the flesh of the Son of Man and drink his blood, you have no life in you" (Jn 6:53). The greatness of his love made him feel hunger. And he said, "I was hungry and you gave me food. If you do not give me food, you cannot enter eternal life" (see Matthew 25:31-46).

Such is Christ's gift. God continues to love the world in our day. He sends you and me to show that he still loves the world and that he has not stopped having mercy on it. It is we who today have to be his love and mercy to the world.

• How tenderly Jesus speaks when he gives himself to his own in Holy Communion. "My flesh is meat indeed and my blood is drink indeed. He that eats my flesh and drinks my blood abides in me and I in him." Oh, what could my Jesus do more than give me his flesh for my food? No, not even God could do more nor show a greater love for me.

*Lord, I am not worthy to receive you...*

• Even Almighty God cannot fill what is already full. We must be empty if we want God to fill us with his fullness. Our Lady had to be empty before she could be full of grace. She had to declare that she was the handmaid of the Lord before God could fill her. So also we must be empty of all pride, all jealousy, of all selfishness before God can fill us with his love.

We must be able to give ourselves so completely to God that he must be able to possess us. We must "Give whatever he takes and take whatever he gives."

How unlike him we are. How little love, how little compassion, how little forgiveness, how little kindness we have. We are not worthy to be so close to him—to enter his heart. For his heart is still open to embrace us. His head is still crowned with thorns, his hands nailed to the cross today.

Let us find out: "Are the nails mine? That spit on his face, is it mine? What part of his body, of his mind, has suffered because of me?" We should ask, not with anxiety or fear, but with a meek and humble heart. Let us find out what part of his body has wounds inflicted by our sin. Let us not go alone but put our hands in his. He is there to forgive seventy times seven. Our Father loves us. He has called us in a special way, given us a name. We belong to him with all our misery, our sin, our weakness, our goodness. We are his.

• Let us not be like the rich young man in the Gospel. Jesus saw him and loved him and wanted him but he had given his heart to something else—to his riches. He was rich, young, and strong. Jesus could not fill him. Instead, be like Zacchaeus. He was a little man—a small man—and he knew his smallness. He recognized his smallness and made a very simple decision in order to see Jesus. He climbed a tree because he knew he was small. If he hadn't opened his heart and responded to Jesus in that simple way, Jesus could not have shown his love, he could not have said, "Come down, Zacchaeus! Come down!" This is the foundation of everything: "Learn of me, that I am meek and humble of heart" (see Matthew 11:29). Be small.

• Complaining and excusing oneself are most natural, but they are a means the devil makes use of to increase our pride. Correction at times hurts most when it is most true.

• Let us really take the trouble to learn the lesson of holiness from Jesus, whose heart was meek and humble. The first lesson from this heart is our examination of conscience, and the rest—love and service—follow at once. Examination is not our work alone, but a partnership between us and Jesus. We should not waste our time in useless looks at our own miseries, but should lift our hearts to God and let his light enlighten us and make him to have his way with us.

• Let's not live distracted lives. Let us know ourselves so that we can better understand our brothers and sisters. If we want to understand those with whom we live, we need to understand ourselves first of all.

• Self-knowledge is very necessary for confession. That is why the saints could say they were wicked criminals. They saw God and then saw themselves—and they saw the difference. Hence they were not surprised when anyone accused them, even falsely. They knew themselves and knew God.

We take hurt because we do not know ourselves, and our eyes are not fixed on God alone; so we do not have real knowledge of God. When the saints looked upon themselves with such horror, they really meant it. They were not pretending.

We must also be able to make the distinction between self-knowledge and sin. Self-knowledge will help us to rise up, whereas sin and the weakness that leads to repeated sin will lead to despondency. Deep confidence and trust will come through self-knowledge. Then you will turn to Jesus to support you in your weakness, whereas if you think you are strong, you will not need our Lord.

• We are convinced that we know each other very well personally. Our lives belong to God—why spend so much time analyzing ourselves?

The problem is not that we don't make our examination of conscience but that we do it by ourselves. We must do it with Christ if it is to be a sincere examination—Jesus is our "Co-worker."

Our souls should be like a transparent crystal through which God can be perceived. This crystal is sometimes covered with dirt and dust. To remove this dust we carry out our examination of conscience, in order to obtain a clean heart.

God will help us to remove that dust, as long as we allow him to, if our will is that his will come about. Perhaps this is what we have lacked.

Our duties, our attitude toward our neighbor, our contacts, can offer us matter for reflection. If we carry out our examination without anything to divert our attention, we will realize that we need Jesus to help us discover our unfaithfulnesses.

Our examination of conscience is the mirror we focus toward nature: a human test, no doubt, but one that needs a mirror in order to faithfully reflect its faults. If we undertake this task with greater faithfulness, perhaps we will realize that what we sometimes consider a stumbling block is rather a rock we can step on.

• You need only ask at night before you go to bed, "What did I do to Jesus today? What did I do for Jesus today? What did I do with Jesus today?" You have only to look at your hands. This is the best examination of conscience.

• Our total surrender will come today by surrendering even our sins so that we will be poor. "Unless you become a child you cannot come to me." You are too big, too heavy; you cannot be lifted up. We need humility to acknowledge our sin. The knowledge of our sin helps us to rise. "I will get up and go to my Father."

*... but only say the word and I shall be healed.*

• Make us worthy, Lord, to serve our brothers and sisters scattered throughout the entire world, who live and die in poverty and hunger. Through the service of our hands, give them their daily bread; and by our understanding love, give them peace and joy.

• Jesus, before his death, gave us his body and blood so that we could live, so that we could have strength, so that we would have life and would be able to drag our cross and follow him step by step.

• The Word of God becomes flesh during the day, during meditation, during Holy Communion, during contemplation, during adoration, during silence. That Word in you, you give to others. It is necessary that the Word live in you, that you understand the Word, that you love the Word, that you live the Word. You will not be able to live that Word unless you give it to others.

• Christ made himself the Bread of Life. He wanted to give himself to us in a very special way—in a simple, tangible way—because it is hard for human beings to love God whom they cannot see.

• When we remember that every morning at Communion we have held in our hands all the holiness of God, we feel more willing to abstain from everything that may stain our purity. Thence flows a sincere and deep respect for our own person—respect also toward others leading us to treat them with sensitivity but likewise abstaining from all disordered sentimentality.

• Holy Communion, as the word itself implies, is the intimate union of Jesus and our soul and body. If we want to have life and have it more abundantly, we must live on the flesh of our Lord. The saints understood so well that they could spend hours in preparation and still more in thanksgiving. This needs no explanation, for who could explain "the depth of the riches of the wisdom and knowledge of God"? "How incomprehensible are his judgments!" cried St. Paul, "And how unsearchable his ways, for who has known the mind of the Lord?"

• Like Mary, let us be full of zeal to go in haste to give Jesus to others. She was full of grace when, at the annunciation, she received Jesus. Like her, we too become full of grace every time we receive Holy Communion. It is the same Jesus whom she received and whom we receive at Mass. As soon as she received him she went with haste to give him to John. For us also, as soon as we receive Jesus in Holy Communion, let us go in haste to give him to our sisters, to our poor, to the sick, to the dying, to the lepers, to the unwanted and the unloved. By this we make Jesus present in the world today.

TWELVE

# *Come, Let Us Bow Down*

Every evening when the Missionaries of Charity return from their work, they gather in their chapel for an unbroken hour of adoration. In the stillness of dusk, they find peace in Christ's presence. Focusing on Jesus alone, they pray in confidence that he is listening, and they grow in their love for God and for each other.

Adoration (sometimes called *Benediction*, or "blessing") is a quiet, personal time of intimacy with Jesus in the presence of the Blessed Sacrament, the bread broken for us.

*Come, let us bow down in worship;*
*let us kneel before the Lord who made us.*
*For he is our God,*
*and we are the people he shepherds,*
*the flock he guides.*

Psalm 95:6-7

• After the sisters have finished their day—carrying out their service of love in the company of Jesus, for the love of Jesus, and through Jesus—we have an hour of prayer and of eucharistic adoration. Throughout the day we have been in contact with Jesus through his image of sorrow in the poor and lepers. When the day ends, we come in contact with him again in the tabernacle by means of prayer.

• The tabernacle is the guarantee that Jesus has set his tent among us.

Every day we sisters have the exposition of the Blessed Sacrament. This has brought a deep change in our lives: we have discovered a deeper love of Christ through the afflicted face of the poor. We have been able to know each other better and to know the poor better too, as a concrete witness of God.

Since we have started this form of worship, we have not diminished our work. We continue to devote to it as much time as before, but with a better understanding. People now accept us better because they are hungry for God. They feel a need not for us but for Jesus.

• I remember when Archbishop Fulton J. Sheen told me that from the day he had been ordained a priest, he had never missed an hour of daily adoration of the Blessed Sacrament.

Up to 1973 we used to have adoration only once a week. In 1973, during the General Chapter of our congregation, there was a unanimous cry, "We want daily adoration of the Blessed Sacrament!"

We have much work to do for the poor. Still we have not had to cut back on our work in order to have that hour of adoration. (Often that is the excuse some people give for not having adoration every day.)

I can tell you I have seen a great change in our congregation from the day we started having adoration every day. Our love for Jesus is more intimate. Our love for each other is more understanding. Our love for the poor is more compassionate. And we have twice as many vocations.

Adoration of the Blessed Sacrament and devotion to the Sacred Heart of Jesus go together. We try to have our lives woven with the Eucharist so that we are more united to the Sacred Heart of Jesus.

More and more young people are coming to our houses for adoration.... Especially in Poland, Yugoslavia, and East Germany, many young people come for adoration. This has changed many, many lives.

In our homes for the dying, we have the Blessed Sacrament. And there is always somebody praying.

• Truly, the tenderness of God's love is most extraordinary. When we look at the cross, we know how much Jesus loved us then. When we look at the tabernacle, we know how much he loves us now.

That's why you should ask your parish priests to give you the joy of having adoration of the Blessed Sacrament at least once a week.

Be alone with Jesus.

Then your hearts will feel the joy that only he can give.

• The hour of adoration before the Blessed Sacrament every day has fostered a greater tenderness and love in us. We owe it all to Jesus in the Blessed Sacrament. We cannot be Co-workers or Missionaries of Charity without an intense life of prayer.

• We must ask for the grace to love one another. As Jesus said, "Love one another as I have loved you" (Jn 15:12). To be capable of doing that, our sisters live a life of prayer and sacrifice. That is why we start our day with prayer, Holy Communion, and meditation. Every evening we also have an hour of worship before the Blessed Sacrament. We have permission from our bishop for this time of adoration before the sacrament. This hour of intimacy with Jesus is something very beautiful. It is the greatest gift that God can give us.

Wherever you find yourself, if you are free and you feel the need for Jesus, we have daily worship from 6:30 to 7:30 P.M. in our homes. You are cordially invited to come. Or if it is more practical, go to your own church. Wherever you find yourself, try to begin doing this. Try to put worship into practice in your life. Be alone with Jesus. You will notice a change in your life, in your family, in your parish, and in your environment.

This is something that we should be concerned about as Co-workers. We need to soak up the tender love of Jesus that our people experience when they sense that God loves them. We need to extend to each and everyone the assurance that God loves them.

• Permit me to give you some advice: begin with the adoration of the Blessed Sacrament as the heart of prayer in your communities. Begin having it weekly, and you will see that soon the young brothers and sisters will ask if you can have it daily. Because as we advance in years, we experience a greater hunger for Jesus. The younger ones will encourage us through their magnificent example of sincere love for Jesus.

• Yesterday, a sister was telling me about some sisters who go to the prison. They take the Blessed Sacrament, and the prison chaplain has started daily adoration for half an hour. To see those prisoners, young boys and men, adoring. They are preparing some of those boys for First Communion. They're hungry for God—they are very hungry for God.

• Every moment of prayer, especially before our Lord in the tabernacle, is a sure positive gain. The time we spend in having our daily audience with God is the most precious part of the whole day.

• If you really want to grow in love, come back to the Eucharist, come back to that adoration.

# PART FOUR

## *"To Work Is to Pray"*

Mother Teresa is known around the world for her work with the dying, the "poorest of the poor," the homeless, the unwanted. In the faces of the poor she sees Jesus, and she serves the poor out of deep love for her Lord. It is impossible to separate Mother Teresa's work from her prayer. One blends imperceptibly into the other, so that her entire day is a single offering to Jesus.

In Part Four we come back to the ancient Benedictine motto: "To pray is to work; to work is to pray." As Mother Teresa talks about her vocation, her work with the poor, and her concern for unwanted children, she also talks about her love for Jesus and God's love for the world. "The work we do is nothing more than a means of transforming our love for Christ into something concrete," she says. Her work is her prayer, her communion with God, her love poem to her beloved Lord.

THIRTEEN

# *I Chose You*

The word *vocation* means "calling." In the Roman Catholic church, the word *vocation* is usually used to denote a calling to the priesthood or to the religious life. Mother Teresa sometimes uses the term that way, but sometimes she uses it a little differently. She believes people are called first and foremost to love Jesus, to belong to him. Only secondarily are they called to do a special work, such as that of the Missionaries of Charity for the poor and the dying.

The call to love Jesus comes to all Christians, not just to those who become clergy or members of religious orders. It is a call we are free to accept or reject. For those who accept God's call, it is a wonderful gift that leads to life, not only for us but also for all those whose lives we touch. The deepest vocation of the church, says Mother Teresa, "is to gather people from every tribe and tongue, and people and nation, redeemed by the blood of Christ, to form God's family of love."

> *You did not choose me,*
> *but I chose you and appointed you*
> *that you should go and bear fruit*
> *and that your fruit should abide....*
>
> John 15:16, RSV

*You did not choose me,*
*but I chose you and appointed you...*

• "I will betroth you to me forever in steadfast love, in mercy. I will betroth you to me in faithfulness" (see Hosea 2:21). Thank God from the depths of your heart that he has chosen you for himself and for life. Why are we here? We must have heard Jesus calling us by name. We are like St. Paul. Once he realized the love of Christ, he cared about nothing else. He did not care whether he was scourged or put into prison. For him, only one thing was important: Jesus Christ.

• The Church is each one of us: you, I. We are the ones who have to know, love, and put ourselves at the service of the poorest.

• God loves me. I'm not here just to fill a place, just to be a number. He has chosen me for a purpose. I know it. He will fulfill it if I don't put an obstacle in his way. He will not force me. God could have forced Our Lady. Jesus could have come just like that. The Holy Spirit could have come. But God wanted Mary to say yes. It is the same with us. God doesn't force us, but he wants us to say yes.

• Our constitution says that "as a sign of our consecration we receive a new name." We vow to give ourselves to God completely, and our new name expresses that vow. Our name is called and we answer: "Lord, you have called me." The moment we stop hearing our name being called we will be separated from him. We can recognize his voice calling our name only in the silence of our hearts. Changing our names shows that we belong not to ourselves but to Jesus.

• Our vocation is to belong to Jesus, to belong with a conviction, not because my vocation is to work with the poor or to be a contemplative, but because I am called to belong to him in the conviction that nothing can separate me from his love.

• All the religious congregations—nuns, priests, even the Holy Father—all have the same vocation: to belong to Jesus. "I have chosen you to be mine." That's our vocation. Our means, how we spend our time, may be different. Our love for Jesus in action is only the means, just like clothes. I wear this, you wear that: it's a means. But vocation is not a means. Vocation, for a Christian, is Jesus.

• By following the vocation of a Missionary of Charity, we stand before the world as ambassadors of peace by preaching the message of love in action that crosses all barriers of nationality, creed, or country.

• I was only twelve years old, living with my parents in Skopje, Yugoslavia, when I first sensed the desire to become a nun. At that time there were some very good priests who helped boys and girls follow their vocation, according to God's call. It was then that I realized that my call was to the poor.

Between twelve and eighteen years of age I lost the desire to become a nun. But at eighteen years of age I decided to leave my home and enter the Sisters of Loreto. Since then I have never had the least doubt that I was right. It was God's will: he made the choice.

The Sisters of Loreto were devoted to teaching, which is a genuine apostolate for Christ. But my specific vocation, within the religious vocation, was for the poorest poor. It was a call from inside my vocation—like a second vocation. It was a command to resign Loreto, where I was happy, in order to serve the poor in the streets.

In 1946, when I was going by train to Darjeeling for some spiritual exercises, I sensed a call to renounce everything in order to follow Christ in the poor suburbs, to serve among the poorest poor. I knew that God wanted something from me.

• We who are espoused to Christ cannot make room for other affections in our heart without provoking God's discontent. God has chosen us, but he also has a right to stop choosing us. He will never do that unless we force him to do so. Do not play with your vocation, because when you want to preserve it you will lack the courage to do it.

• How great your vocation is! How happy many would be if they were offered the opportunity to serve personally the king of the world! Well, that is what we are doing. We can touch, serve, and love Christ every day of our lives.

• A vocation is a gift of Christ. He has said, "I have chosen you." Every vocation must really belong to Christ. The work that we are called to accomplish is just a means to give concrete substance to our love for God.

Young women today are seeking something to which they can commit everything. They are convinced that a life of poverty, of prayer, of sacrifice—which will be of help to them in the service of their neighbor, of the poorest poor—is the answer to their desires, their aspirations, their hopes.

I think they see in our congregation this life of poverty, of prayer, and of sacrifice. In our work on behalf of the poorest poor they see carried into action the Lord's words, "I was hungry and you fed me; I was naked and you clothed me; I was homeless and you welcomed me" (see Matthew 25: 35, 36). This is what we, in the anguish and sorrow of the poor, try to do for Christ.

• Our vocation is nothing else but to belong to Christ. The work that we do is only a means to put our love for Christ into living action.

• We all have been called by God. "I have called you by your name," Jesus said. "You are mine. No harm will come to you. You are precious in my sight. I love you." God sends you to be his tenderness and love to his people. If you love Christ, it will be easy for you to fully belong to Jesus and to give Jesus to everyone you find.

• Our sisters and our brothers are called Missionaries of Charity. They are young people who are called to be the carriers of God's love.

• The greatest gift that God can bestow on a family is to choose a son or a daughter for himself. You should encourage this, but it will not be possible for you if you don't pray. Let us pray then. Let's not pray long, drawn-out prayers, but let's pray short ones full of love. Prayer unites us with Christ. Simply open your hearts to him. Also, simply accept what he sends you. With a big smile, generously give him what he asks of you. You will soon realize that this is the best prayer that you can offer in your families. God will do the rest, never fear. Where God is, there is love; and where there is love, there always is an openness to serve.

• We are not social workers. Our vocation is to belong to Jesus. He has chosen us for himself alone. What we do for the poorest of the poor is nothing more than to put into practice our love for Christ, like a living parable.

**Q:** *What will happen, Mother, when you are no longer with us?*
**MT:** I believe that if God finds a person even more useless than me, he will do even greater things through her because this work is his. I am sure that the sisters will work with the same energy. As long as they remain faithful to their poverty and to the Eucharist, they will be faithful to the poor. There is no reason to worry. There is nothing to fear. God has always found someone, just like he found me.

• We have a great deal of worth in the eyes of God. I never tire of saying over and over again that God loves us. In the Constitution of the Missionaries of Charity, we have a beautiful statement about chastity. It says, "Jesus offers his lifelong, faithful, and personal friendship, embracing us in tenderness and love." It is a wonderful thing that God himself loves me tenderly. That is why we should have courage, joy, and the conviction that nothing can separate us from the love of Christ.

• Something happened to one of the sisters who was sent to study. The day she was to receive her degree she died. When she was dying she asked, "Why did Jesus call me for such a short time?" And her superior answered, "Jesus wants you, not your works." She was perfectly happy after that.

• Your vows are nothing but worship of God. If you are sincere in your prayers, then your vows have meaning; otherwise, they will mean nothing. The taking of your vows is also a prayer because it is worship of God. Your vows are between you and God alone. There is no one in between. It is all between Jesus and you.

• To be a Co-worker is a gift from God. It is not simply a title. It means to be an active co-worker with Christ. The name of "Mother Teresa" is frequently referred to in our work, but really you and I are co-workers with Christ. That is why I say that being a Co-worker is a gift from God. It is a hidden grace. We don't see it, but it is really a gift from God. Why has God chosen you? Why me? This is a mystery.

• What delicate love God has had for the poor of the world to have created the Missionaries of Charity. You and I have been called by our name, because he loved us. Because you and I are somebody special to him—to be his heart to love him in the poor, his hands to serve him in the poorest of the poor. My children, how much love and care we must take of him—if only we were in love with him. Let us learn to pray the work, to be able to be twenty-four hours with Jesus, to do it for Jesus and to Jesus. We need a pure heart, a heart that is filled with nothing but Jesus.

• Young people, with your lives you determine the outcome of his call to you. Will you accept it? It is a call to you and me. Every Christian soul is called to belong to God, some in a special way through the priesthood and the religious life.

• You, young men, whom Jesus has called, whom Jesus has chosen for his own, consider the call to be that bridge that can link souls to God.

• You must not be afraid to say "Yes" to Jesus, because there is no greater love than his love and no greater joy than his joy. My prayer for you is that you come to understand and have the courage to answer Jesus' call to you with the simple word Yes.

***... that you should go and bear fruit***
***and that your fruit should abide.***

• Our eucharistic union with Christ should bear fruit, since Jesus has said, "I am the vine, you are the branches" (Jn 15:5, RSV). Grapes are in the branches, not on the stalk. How great then is your responsibility and mine, the responsibility of us all, since the fruit will depend on the union of the branches to the vine!

• Our spiritual life is a life of reliance on God. Its fruit is the work for the poor. Our work is our prayer because we carry it out through Jesus, in Jesus, and for the sake of Jesus.

• As you know, we have got our brothers also who are Missionaries of Charity. One of our brothers loves the lepers. We are taking care of forty-nine thousand lepers in India. This brother really loves the lepers. He came one day after he had had some difficulties with his superior. He said to me, "I love the lepers; I want to be with them. I want to work for them. My vocation is to be with the lepers." I said to him, "Brother, you are making a mistake. Your vocation is not to work for the lepers. Your vocation is to belong to Jesus. The work for the lepers is only your love for Christ in action; and, therefore, it makes no difference to anyone as long as you are doing it to him, as long as you are doing it with him. That's all that matters. That is the completion of your vocation, of your belonging to Christ."

• We shall go freely in the name of Jesus, to towns and villages all over the world, even amid squalid and dangerous surroundings, with Mary the immaculate mother of Jesus, seeking out the spiritually poorest of the poor with God's own tender affection and proclaiming to them the good news of salvation and hope, singing with them his songs, bringing to them his love, peace, and joy.

We shall call sinners to repentance, and turn them to God by our personal concern for them, proclaim to them the mercy of God, and when necessary remind them also of the justice of God, and teach them the way to salvation through abnegation and the cross, through a total change of mind and heart, through belief in the name of Jesus, and through living his message of love for the Father and one's neighbor.

We shall instruct the ignorant by the power of the example of our lives lived entirely in and with Jesus Christ our Lord, bearing witness to the truth of the gospel by our single-minded devotion to and burning love of Christ and his Church, and also by verbal proclamation of the Word of God fearlessly, openly, and clearly, according to the teaching of the Church, whenever opportunity offers.

We shall counsel the doubtful by listening to them attentively, lovingly, and prayerfully and then speaking to them the truth of God, firmly, gently, and with love.

We shall sustain the tempted by our prayer, penance, and understanding love and when opportunity offers also by enlightening and encouraging words.

We shall befriend the friendless and comfort the sick and sorrowful by our real love and personal concern for them, identifying ourselves with them in their pain and sorrow and by praying with them for God's healing and comfort and by encouraging them to offer their sufferings to the Lord for the salvation of the whole world.

We shall bear wrongs patiently by offering no resistance to the wicked—if anyone hits us on the right cheek by turning the left also; if anyone takes away anything from us by not trying to get it back.

We shall forgive injuries by seeking no revenge but returning good for evil, by loving our enemies and praying for those who persecute us and blessing those who curse us.

We shall bring prayer into the lives of the spiritually poorest of the poor by praying with them and for them and making them personally experience the power of prayer and the reality of the promise of Jesus, "Ask and you shall receive. Whatever you ask in my name I will do."

• The missionary aspect of our call to contemplation will find its expression in going in haste to the spiritually poorest of the poor personally, to proclaim the peace, joy, and love of God wherever we are sent.

In spirit, to every part of the vast creation of God from the furthest planet to the depths of the sea; from one abandoned convent chapel to another abandoned church; from an abortion clinic in one city to a prison cell in another; from the source of a river in one continent to a lonely mountain cave in another, and even into heaven and the gates of hell, praying with and for each of God's creation to save and sanctify each one for whom the blood of the Son of God has been shed.

• We deliberately renounce all desires to see the fruit of our labor, doing all we can as best we can, leaving the rest in the hands of God.

• If someone feels that God wants from him a transformation of social structures, that's an issue between him and his God. We all have the duty to serve God where we feel called. I feel called to help individuals, to love each human being. It is not my task to judge institutions—I am not competent to judge anybody. I never think in terms of crowds in general but in terms of persons. Were I to think about crowds, I would never begin anything. It is the person that matters. I believe in person-to-person encounters.

• In the world there are some who struggle for justice and human rights. We have no time for this because we are in daily and continuous contact with men who are starving for a piece of bread to put in their mouth and for some affection. Should I devote myself to struggle for the justice of tomorrow or even for the justice of today, the most needy people would die right in front of me because they lack a glass of milk.

Nevertheless, I want to state clearly that I do not condemn those who struggle for justice. I believe there are different options for the people of God. To me, the most important is to serve the neediest people.

Within the church some do one thing, others do a different thing. What is important is that all of us remain united, each one of us developing his own specific task.

• The very fact that God has placed a soul on our way is a sign that he wants us to do something for it.

• The vow of charity is a fruit of our union with Christ, just as a child is the fruit of the sacrament of matrimony. Just as a lamp cannot burn without oil, so also a vow of charity cannot live without the vows of poverty and obedience.

• The particular aim of our congregation is to offer wholehearted free service to the poorest poor, to Christ in the semblance of those who suffer. The work we carry out is only our love for Christ in concrete action. That is why we strive to love Christ—

—with an undivided love in chastity;
—through the freedom of poverty;
—in total submission in obedience;
—and in cordial service to the poorest poor;
—to Christ under the semblance of those who suffer.

These are the four vows we proclaim, and they make the essential difference in our life.

• Pope Paul says that vocation means the capacity to heed the imploring voices of the world of innocent souls of those who suffer, who have no comfort, no guidance, no love. This requirement is beautifully fulfilled by our vow of wholehearted and free service to the poor. Just as Christ went about doing good, healing the sick, casting out devils, preaching the kingdom of God, we too spend ourselves untiringly in seeking, in towns as well as villages, even amid the dustbins, the poor, the abandoned, the sick, the infirm, the dying, and in taking care of them, helping them, visiting them, and giving them the message of Christ, and trying our best to bring them to God.

• If something belongs to me, I've got full power to use it as I want. I belong to Jesus; he can do to me whatever he wants. The work is not our vocation. I can do this work without being a religious. Can you tell me why we become Missionaries of Charity? The work is not our vocation. Our vocation is to belong to him....

• We are called the "Missionaries of Charity."

A missionary is one sent with a mission—a message to deliver. Just as Jesus was sent by his Father, we too are sent by him and filled with his Spirit to be witnesses of his gospel of love and compassion, first in our communities and then in our apostolate among the poorest of the poor all over the world.

As missionaries we must be—

— carriers of God's love, ready to go in haste, like Mary, in search of souls;
— burning lights that give light to all men;
— the salt of the earth;
— souls consumed with one desire: Jesus. We must keep his interests continually in our hearts and minds, carrying our Lord to places where he has not walked before;
— fearless in doing the things he did, courageously going through danger and death with him and for him;
— ready to accept joyously the need to die daily if we want to bring souls to God, to pay the price he paid for souls;
— ever ready to go to any part of the world and to respect and appreciate unfamiliar customs of other peoples, their living conditions and language, willing to adapt ourselves if and when necessary;
— happy to undertake any labor and toil, and glad to make any sacrifice involved in our missionary life.

• Persuaded of our nothingness and with the blessing of obedience we attempt all things, doubting nothing, for with God all things are possible.

We will allow the good God to make plans for the future, for yesterday has gone, tomorrow has not yet come, and we have only today to make him known, loved, and served.

Grateful for the thousands of opportunities Jesus gives us to bring hope into a multitude of lives by our concern for the individual sufferer, we will help our troubled world at the brink of despair to discover a new reason to live or to die with a smile of contentment on its lips.

We do not allow ourselves to be disheartened by any failure as long as we have done our best. Neither do we glory in our success, but refer all to God in deepest thankfulness.

• As a religious community, modeled on the first Christian community, our first great responsibility is to be community, revealing first to one another something of God's own love, concern, and tenderness—what it means to know and to be known, to love and to be loved, and thus to be a sign witnessing to the deepest vocation of the church, which is to gather people from every tribe and tongue, and people and nation, redeemed by the blood of Christ, to form God's family of love. "See how they love each other."

• No Missionary of Charity is called to do big things. Our work sounds big because there are so many little things, but when you look at it, there is nothing to show—nothing. I was so happy to see a sister cleaning the toilets, because they were shining. She must have cleaned them with great love and done it in the presence of God.

• You are being sent; you have not chosen for yourself where you want to go; and you are sent just as Jesus was sent to us. You are sent not to teach but to learn: learn to be meek and humble of heart. You are sent to serve and not to be served: Go to serve with a humble heart. Never escape the hard work. Be always the first one to do it.

• We Missionaries of Charity take a special vow to God to give wholehearted, free service to the poorest of the poor. We have no income, no Church assistance, no government salary, no government grants. We have none of that. And yet we deal with thousands and thousands and thousands of people, and we have never had to say to anybody, "We're sorry, we have run out of supplies."

• To work without love is slavery.

• We will be very blessed to have the joy this love brings of working together and making our work a prayer:

With Jesus, for Jesus, to Jesus.

With God, for God, to God.

That way we are praying to God, not just doing our work.

When you are cooking, washing clothes, working hard in the office, do it all with joy. That will be your love for God in action!

• The difference between our work and social work is that we give wholehearted, free service for the love of God. In the beginning, when the work started, I got a fever and had a dream about St. Peter. He said to me, "No, there is no place for you here. No slums in heaven." "All right," I answered him, "then I shall go on working. I'll bring the people from the slums to heaven."

• Our vocation is not the work—the fidelity to humble works is our means to put our love into action.

• What have we to learn? To be meek and humble; if we are meek and humble we will learn to pray. If we learn to pray, we will belong to Jesus. If we belong to Jesus we will learn to believe, and if we believe we will learn to love, and if we love we will learn to serve.

• Spend your time in prayer. If you pray you will have faith, and if you have faith you will naturally want to serve. The one who prays cannot but have faith, and when you have faith you want to put it into action. Faith in action is service. Faith in action becomes a delight because it gives you the opportunity of putting your love for Christ into action—it is meeting Christ, serving Christ.

• You need especially to pray, for in our society, the work is only the fruit of prayer, our love in action. If you are really in love with Christ, no matter how small the work, it will be done better; it will be wholehearted. If your work is slapdash, then your love for God is slapdash. Your work must prove your love.

• We must work in great faith, steadily, efficiently, and above all with great love and cheerfulness, for without this our work will be only the work of slaves, serving a hard master.

• However beautiful the work is, be detached from it—even ready to give it up. You may be doing great good in one place, but obedience calls you elsewhere. Be ready to leave. The work is not yours. You are working for Jesus.

• You may be exhausted with work—you may even kill yourself—but unless your work is interwoven with love, it is useless.

• Don't give in to discouragement. No more must you do so when you try to settle a marriage crisis or convert a sinner and don't succeed. If you are discouraged, it is a sign of pride because it shows you trust in your own powers. Never bother about people's opinions. Be humble and you will never be disturbed. It is very difficult in practice because we all want to see the result of our work. Leave it to Jesus.

• Never do the work carelessly because you wish to hide your gifts. Remember, the work is his. You are his co-worker. Therefore, he depends on you for that special work. Do the work with him, and the work will be done for him. The talents God has given you are not yours—they have been given to you for your use, for the glory of God. There can be no half-measures in the work. You may feel very bad, but feelings are not the measure of our love for Christ. It is our will and our work that matters. Be great and use everything in you for the good Master.

• You have done a lot of work these days; it was nicely done, but did you give what was inside of you?

What did that giving mean to you? Did you give with love and respect? If you did not pray that giving, it was just a giving of self.

Did the people see you give with love and respect? Did you give the medicine with faith to the sick Christ? This is the difference between you and the social worker.

• The more repugnant the work, the greater the effect of love and cheerful service. If I had not first picked up that woman who was eaten by rats—her face, and legs, and so on—I could not have been a

Missionary of Charity. But I returned, picked her up, and took her to Camphel Hospital. If I had not, the Society would have died. Feelings of repugnance are human. If we give our wholehearted, free service in spite of such feelings, we will become holy. St. Francis of Assisi was repulsed by lepers but he overcame it. He died; but Christ lives.

• Today, in the words of our Holy Father, each one of us must be able "to cleanse what is dirty, to warm what is lukewarm, to strengthen what is weak, to enlighten what is dark." We must not be afraid to proclaim Christ's love and to love as he loved. In the work we have to do, no matter how small and humble it may be, we must make it Christ's love in action. Do not be afraid to proclaim his poverty. Do not be afraid to go with Christ and be subject to those who have authority from above and so declare Christ's obedience unto death. Rejoice that once more Christ is walking through the world, in you and through you, going about doing good.

• If you are put in the kitchen, you must not think it does not require brains—that sitting, standing, coming, going, anything will do. God will not ask that sister how many books she has read; how many miracles she has worked; but he will ask her if she has done her best, for the love of him. Can she in all sincerity say, "I have done my best"? Even if the best is failure, it must be our best, our utmost.

• The contemplative and apostolic fruitfulness of our way of life depends on our being rooted in Christ Jesus our Lord by our deliberate choice of small and simple means for the fulfillment of our mission and by our fidelity to humble work of love among the spiritually poorest, identifying ourselves with them, sharing their poverty and insecurities until it hurts.

• We need prayers in order to better carry out the work of God. Pray for us, so that the work we do may be God's work and so that in every moment we may know how to be completely available to him.

# FOURTEEN

## *Blessed Are You Who Are Poor*

Mother Teresa is never condescending or pitying when she speaks of the poor. To the contrary, she has a positive, vibrant love for poor people. "See the greatness of the poor!" she exclaims after telling a story about a poor person who was especially generous or grateful or loving.

In order to serve the poor, the Missionaries of Charity become poor themselves. They serve as equals, as friends, of the people they serve. In doing this, they follow the example of Jesus, who became poor for humanity's sake.

Mother Teresa often speaks to affluent audiences in developed countries. To these people she emphasizes that poverty means more than lack of money. People who are financially comfortable can know loneliness and neglect and abuse. The poor, she warns, may be in our own homes.

The Missionaries of Charity offer more than food and shelter. They offer the kingdom of God, where all needs are satisfied and where people are rich in laughter.

*Blessed are the poor in spirit,*
*for theirs is the kingdom of heaven.*
*Blessed are those who mourn, for they shall be comforted....*
*Blessed are those who hunger and thirst...*
*they shall be satisfied.*

Matthew 5:3-6, RSV

*Blessed are the poor in spirit*
*for theirs is the kingdom of heaven.*

• To the world it seems foolish that we delight in poor food, that we relish rough and insipid bulgur; possess only three sets of habits made of coarse cloth or old soutanes, mend and patch them, take great care of them and refuse to have extra; enjoy walking in any shape and color of shoes; bathe with just a bucket of water in small bathing rooms; sweat and perspire but refuse to have a fan; go hungry and thirsty but refuse to eat in the houses of the people; refuse to have radios or gramophones which could be relaxing to the racked nerves after the whole day's hard toil; walk distances in the rain and hot summer sun, or go cycling, travel by second-class tram, or third-class overcrowded trains; sleep on hard beds, giving up soft and thick mattresses which would be soothing to the aching bodies after the whole day's hard work; kneel on the rough and thin carpets in the chapel, giving up soft and thick ones; delight in lying in the common wards in the hospital among the poor of Christ when we could easily have private cabins; work like coolies at home and outside when we could easily employ servants and do only the light jobs; relish cleaning the toilets and dirt in the Nirmal Hriday and Shishu Bhavan as though that was the most beautiful job in the world and call it all a tribute to God. To them we are wasting our precious life and burying our talents. Yes, our lives are utterly wasted if we use only the light of reason. Our life has no meaning unless we look at Christ in his poverty.

• Our Lord gives us a living example: From the very first day of his human existence he was brought up in a poverty which no human being will ever be able to experience, because "being rich he made himself poor." As I am his co-worker, his "alter Christus," I must be brought up and nourished by that poverty which our Lord asks of me.

• A rich man of Delhi, in speaking of our Society, said, "How wonderful it is to see sisters so free from the world—in the twentieth century when one thinks everything is old-fashioned but the present day." Keep to the simple ways of poverty: of repairing your shoes, and so on—of loving poverty as you love your mother.

• God has not created poverty; it is we who have created it. Before God, all of us are poor.

• God needs our poverty, not our abundance.

• I think that if today there are no vocations in the Church, or if they are scarce, it is partly due to the fact that there is too much wealth, too much comfort, too high a standard of living, not only in families but even in religious life.

From all parts of the world young people are coming to India to take on a very poor life, poorer than ours. They are driven by the desire to be free from their environment of wealth. I think they want to be a living example of Christ's poverty.

It is not enough to know the spirit of poverty; you have to know poverty itself. Poverty means not having anything. Today everyone, even those who come from well-do-do environments, wants to know what it really means to have nothing.

Most of the vocations we receive come from Europe and America. They have asked to join the congregation not because of the work but because of a love for poverty.

• Riches, both material and spiritual, can choke you if you do not use them fairly. Let us remain as empty as possible so that God can fill us up. For not even God can put anything in a heart that is already full. God does not impose himself on us.

• When one comes in touch with money, one loses contact with God. May God keep us from that; death is to be preferred.

What can be done with surplus money? Invest it in the bank? No, let us not fall into the habits of the moneylender. We have not the least reason for that, for God is watching over us.

One day there springs up the desire for money and for all that money can provide—the superfluous, luxury in eating, luxury in dressing, trifles. Needs increase because one thing calls for another. The result is uncontrollable dissatisfaction.

If you have to go shopping, pick up the simplest things. We have to be happy with our poverty. Let us not be driven by our small egotisms.

It may happen that we have to carry water up to a given floor for a bath and that we find three full buckets; the temptation then comes to use all of the water.

If you have to sleep in a poorly ventilated facility, do not give signs of suffocation or difficult breathing, so as to give the impression that you are uncomfortable. It is there that poverty lies.

Poverty makes us free. Therefore we are to rejoice, smile, and have a cheerful heart.

• The poor are wonderful people. They have their own dignity, which we can easily see. Usually the poor are not known, and therefore one is not able to discover their dignity. But the poor have above all great courage to lead the life they lead. They are forced to live like that; poverty has been imposed on them. We choose poverty; they are forced to accept it.

• On the cross Christ was deprived of everything. The cross itself had been given him by Pilate; the nails and the crown, by the soldiers. He was naked.

When he died he was stripped of the cross, the nails, and the crown. He was wrapped in a piece of canvas donated by a charitable soul, and he was buried in a tomb that did not belong to him.

Despite all that, Jesus could have died like a king and could even have been spared death. He chose poverty because he knew that it was the genuine means to possess God and to bring his love to the earth.

• It would be a shame for us to be richer than Jesus, who for our sake endured poverty.

• Our beautiful work with and for the poor is a privilege and a gift for us. St. Vincent de Paul used to tell the young aspirants to his order, "Remember, the poor are our masters. We must love and obey them." I think that if we go to the poor with that love, with only the desire to give God to them, to bring the joy of Christ (which is our strength) into their homes; if they look at us and see Jesus and his love and compassion in us—I think the world will soon be full of peace and love.

• Our sisters and brothers work for the poorest of the poor—the sick, the dying, the lepers, the abandoned children. But I can tell you that in all these years I have never heard the poor grumble or curse, nor have I seen any of them dejected with sadness. The poor are great people, they can accept very difficult things.

• Poverty is freedom. It is a freedom so that what I possess doesn't own me, so that what I possess doesn't hold me down, so that my possessions don't keep me from sharing or giving of myself.

• When we opened our home in New York, the late Terence Cardinal Cooke was very concerned about the prospect of having to send us a fixed amount every month for the livelihood of the sisters. He was a man who loved the sisters very much. I didn't want to hurt his feelings, but I found it very hard to explain to him that we work only for the love of God. We simply couldn't accept any fixed amount for our living expenses. I explained to him the only way that I could. I told him, "Your Eminence, I don't think God is going to go bankrupt here in New York."

**Q:** *If God created the world, why does he allow such a degree of poverty to exist?*

**MT:** God created the world and saw that it was good. God created man and saw that he was good. God created everything, and he realized that each thing was good. How can we complain against God for the poverty and suffering that exist in the world? Can we honestly do so? God saw that everything was good. What we do with things is another matter.

• Our poverty is our dowry.

With regard to God, our poverty is our humble recognition and acceptance of our sinfulness, helplessness and utter nothingness, and the acknowledgement of our neediness before him, which expresses itself as hope in him, as an openness to receive all things from him as from our Father.

Our poverty should be true gospel poverty—gentle, tender, glad and openhearted, always ready to give an expression of love. Poverty is love before it is renunciation. To love, it is necessary to give. To give, it is necessary to be free from selfishness.

• Desirous to share Christ's own poverty and that of our poor—
- —we acccept to have everything in common and to share with one another in the Society;
- —we do not accept anything whatsoever from our parents, friends, or benefactors for our personal use. Whatever is given to us is handed over to our superiors for the common use of the community or for the work;
- —we shall eat the food of the people, of the country where we live, using what is cheapest. It should be sufficient and wholesome so as to maintain good health which is essential for the work of our vocation;
- —our Houses should be simple and modest, places where the poor feel at home;
- —we shall walk whenever opportunity offers, in order to take the cheapest means of transport available;
- —we shall sleep in common dormitories without privacy like the poor;
- —we and our poor will depend entirely on Divine Providence both for our material and spiritual needs.

• Poverty is necessary because we are working with the poor. When they complain about the food, we can say: we eat the same. They say, "It was so hot last night, we could not sleep." We can reply, "We also felt very hot." The poor have to wash for themselves, go barefoot; we do the same. We have to go down and lift them up. It opens the heart of the poor when we can say we live the same way they do. Sometimes they only have one bucket of water. It is the same with us. The poor have to stand in line; we do too. Food, clothing, everything must be like that of the poor. We have no fasting. Our fasting is to eat the food as we get it.

• Christ being rich emptied himself. This is where contradiction lies. If I want to be poor like Christ—who became poor even though he was rich—I must do the same.

Nowadays people want to be poor and live with the poor, but they want to be free to dispose of things as they wish. To have this freedom is to be rich. They want both and they cannot have both. This is another kind of contradiction.

Our poverty is our freedom. This is our poverty—the giving up of our freedom to dispose of things, to choose, to possess. The moment I use and dispose of things as mine, that moment I cease to be poor.

• We practice the virtue of poverty when we mend our clothes quickly and as beautifully as we can. To go about in a torn habit and sari is certainly not the sign of the virtue of poverty. For, remember, we do not profess the poverty of beggars, but the poverty of Christ. Let us also remember that our body is the temple of the Holy Spirit, and for that reason we must respect it always with neatly mended clothes.

We would never dream of using dirty, torn cloth as a tabernacle veil to cover the door of the dwelling that Christ chose for himself on earth since his Ascension into heaven. In the same way, we should never cover the temple of the Holy Spirit, which is our body, with torn, dirty, untidy clothes. Patched clothes are no disgrace. It is said of St. Francis of Assisi that when he died his habit had so many patches that the original cloth was no longer there.

• I will never forget something that happened when I was at Loreto. One of the children was very, very naughty. She was only six or seven years old. One day, when she was extremely naughty, I took her hand and said, "Come, we're going for a walk." She had some money with her. One hand held my hand and the other held tightly to the money. "I will buy this, I will buy that," she kept saying. Suddenly she saw a blind beggar, and at once she left the money with him. From that day she was a completely different child. She had been so small and so naughty. Yet that one decision changed her life. It is the same with you. Get rid of anything that's holding you back. If you want to be all for Jesus, the decision has to come from within you.

• The poor do not need our compassion or our pity; they need our help. What they give to us is more than what we give to them.

• We have no right to judge the rich. For our part, what we desire is not a class struggle but a class encounter, in which the rich save the poor and the poor save the rich.

We favor making the poor responsible. We ask their collaboration; we invite them to look for solutions themselves.

In Calcutta there are poor people who survive by serving in the houses of those who have more. They even come to offer their work gratis to our centers, perhaps for just a half-hour each week. This is a way of putting themselves at the level of the rest of men.

• The indifference of people who walk by without picking up those whom we pick up is a confirmation of their ignorance and lack of faith.

If they were convinced that the one who is lying on the ground is their brother or their sister, I think they would undoubtedly do something. Unfortunately, they do not know what compassion is, and they do not know those beings.

If they understood them, they would immediately become aware of the greatness of those human beings who are lying on the side-walks. They would love them naturally, and loving them would lead them to serve them.

I can assert that those who really commit themselves to knowing the poor soon realize that the poor are our brothers, no matter what their race, nationality, or religion.

• The aim of the Missionaries of Charity is to take God, to take his love, to the homes of the poor and thus to lead them to him. It does not matter who they are, nor what their nationality or social status may be. We intend to make them understand the love and compassion that God has for them, which is a love of predilection.

**Q:** *What advice would you give to the people of today?*
**MT:** Know the poorest of the poor among your neighbors, in your neighborhoods, in your town, in your city, perhaps in your own family. When you know them, that will lead you to love them. And love will impel you to serve them. Only then will you begin to act like Jesus and live out the gospel. Place yourselves at the service of the poor. Open your hearts to love them. Be living witnesses of God's mercy. This may lead you to give up your own sons so that they may serve God, who gives preference to the poor.

• The poorest of the poor, irrespective of caste, creed, or nationality are—

— the hungry, the thirsty, the naked, the homeless, the ignorant, the captives, the crippled, the leprosy sufferers, the alcoholics, the sick and dying destitutes, the unloved, the abandoned, the outcasts; all those who are a burden to human society, who have lost all hope and faith in life; and every Missionary of Charity, by accepting to live the life of evangelical poverty and by the very fact of being sinners;

— and all hard-hearted, persistent sinners; those under the power of the evil one; those who are leading others to sin, error or confusion; the atheists, the erring; those in confusion and doubt; the tempted, the spiritually blind, the weak, lax, and ignorant; those not yet touched by the light of Christ; those hungry for the Word and peace of God; the difficult, the repulsive, the rejected, the sorrowful, and the souls in purgatory.

• As you love God you must love the poor in their sufferings. The love of the poor overflows from your love for God. You must find the poor and serve them. When you have found them, you must take them to your heart. We owe our people the greatest gratitude, because they allow us to touch Christ. We must love the poor like we love him. A Hindu told me, "I know what you do in Nirmal Hriday, you take them from the streets and bring them to heaven."

• Jesus said, "Go and teach all nations" (see Matthew 28:19). In every country there are poor. On certain continents poverty is more spiritual than material. That poverty consists of loneliness, discouragement, and the lack of meaning in life. I have also seen in Europe and America very poor people sleeping on newspapers or rags in the streets. There are those kind of poor in London, Madrid, and Rome. My visits have the sole purpose of making people aware of the poor in their own countries. It is too easy simply to talk or concern ourselves with the poor who are far away. It is much harder and, perhaps, more challenging to turn our attention and concern toward the poor who live right next door to us.

• All over the world people are saying that Mother Teresa is spoiling the poor by giving them things free. At a seminary in Bangalore, once a nun said to me, "Mother Teresa, you are spoiling the poor people by giving them things free. They are losing their human dignity." When everyone was quiet, I said calmly, "No one spoils as much as God himself. See the wonderful gifts he has given us freely. All of you here have no glasses, yet you all can see. If God were to take money for your sight, what would happen? Continually we are breathing and living on oxygen that we do not pay for. What would happen if God were to say, 'If you work four hours, you will get sunshine for two hours'? How many of us would then survive?" Then I also told them: "There are many congregations who spoil the rich; it is good to have one congregation in the name of the poor, to spoil the poor." There was profound silence; nobody said a word after that.

*Blessed are those who mourn, for they shall be comforted.*

• We know that poverty means, first of all, to be hungry for bread, to need clothing, and not have a home. But there is a far greater kind of poverty. It means being unwanted, unloved, and neglected. It means having no one to call your own.

• It's possible that in the apartment or house across from yours, there is someone who is blind. Perhaps there is a blind man who would be thrilled if you would go over and read the newspaper to him. It's possible that there is a family that needs something that seems insignificant to you, something as simple as having someone babysit their child for half an hour. There are so many little things that are so small many people almost forget about them. But for you, as sons and daughters of charity, these aren't small things. They show your love for Christ. And this is what I am asking of you. Place yourselves at the service of the poor. Above all, do it right where you are and love them from the heart.

• In Haiti—just as in England, Spain, Italy, or India—there are unhappy people everywhere. Not only because they don't have any bread to eat. No, they hunger for love, understanding, and companionship. They suffer from loneliness, the feeling of being unwanted and rejected, a poverty of the soul. These are the things that can be far worse than being hungry or not having enough material goods.

In Western countries, your countries, I can perceive this in the people I meet. There exists something in common among your poor and the poor in India: the need for happiness and joy in spite of the hardships of life. It is something marvelous that the same call unites us, so that we can together extend Jesus' saving work.

• You must experience the joy of poverty. Poverty is not only renunciation. Poverty is joy. Poverty is love. My reason for doing without is that I love Jesus. Unless you experience for yourself this joy of poverty, you will never understand what I am saying.

• I want you to experience that joy of poverty which is really the perfect joy of St. Francis of Assisi. He called it Lady Poverty. St. Ignatius called it Mother Poverty. The more we have, the less we can give. So let us have less to be able to give all to Jesus.

• Do we know our poor people? Do we know the poor in our house, in our family? Perhaps they are not hungry for a piece of bread. Perhaps our children, husband, wife, are not hungry, or naked, or dispossessed, but are you sure there is no one there who feels unwanted, deprived of affection? Where is your elderly father or mother?

One day I visited a house where our sisters shelter the aged. This is one of the nicest houses in England, filled with beautiful and precious things, yet there was not one smile on the faces of those people. All of them were looking toward the door.

I asked the sister in charge, "Why are they like that? Why can you not see a smile on their faces?" (I am accustomed to seeing smiles on people's faces. I think a smile generates a smile, just as love generates love.)

The sister answered, "The same thing happens every day. They are always waiting for someone to come and visit them. Loneliness eats them up, and day after day they do not stop looking. Nobody comes."

Abandonment is an awful poverty.

• There are poor people everywhere, but the deepest poverty is not being loved. The poor whom we must seek may live near us or far away. They can be materially or spiritually poor. They may be hungry for bread or hungry for friendship. They may need clothing, or they may need the sense of wealth that God's love for them represents. They may need the shelter of a house made of bricks and cement or the shelter of having a place in our hearts.

• Our sisters are working in New York with the shut-ins. They see the terrible pain of our people, the pain of loneliness, of fear, of being unwanted and unloved. I think it is much greater pain, much greater than even cancer or tuberculosis. The sisters have often met people like that, people who are completely brokenhearted, desperate with feelings of hurt.

• You in the West have the spiritually poorest of the poor much more than you have physically poor people. Very often among the rich there are very, very spiritually poor people. I find it is not difficult to give a plate of rice to a hungry person, to furnish a bed to a person who has no bed, but to console or to remove that bitterness, to remove that anger, to remove that loneliness takes a long time.

*... Blessed are those who hunger and thirst...*
*they shall be satisfied.*

• There is a natural conscience in every human being to know right from wrong. I deal with thousands who are non-Christians, and you can see such a conscience at work in their lives, drawing them to God. In everybody there is a tremendous hunger for God, in spite of all appearances.

• Christ certainly did not feast sumptuously during his life. His parents were poor, and the poor do not feast on the good things of the table. In fact he often endured real want, as the multiplication of the loaves and fishes and the plucking of the ears of grain on walks through the fields teach us. The thought of these instances should be salutary reminders when our meals are meager in the mission or at home. If dishes taste good, thank God; if not, thank him still and thank him even more because he has given you an opportunity to imitate our Savior in his poverty. It would be a defect to speak about food or to complain about what is served; to be occupied with such thoughts at any time is not edifying.

• St. Thérèse of Lisieux said, "Our Lord has need of our love. He has no need of our works. The same God who declares that he has no need to tell us if he be hungry, did not disdain to beg a little water from the Samaritan woman. He was thirsty, but when he said, 'Give me to drink,' he, the creator of the universe, asked for the love of his creature. He thirsted for love."

• Today the world is hungry for God. You and I can bring him to others, as long as we ourselves have understood the love of Christ.

• I remember the day I picked up a woman in the street, thinking that she was starving to death. I offered her a dish of rice. She kept looking at it for a long while. I tried to persuade her to eat.

Then she said, with utter simplicity, "I can't believe it's rice. I have been a long time without eating."

She condemned no one. She did not complain against the rich. She did not utter any bitter words. She simply couldn't believe it was rice.

• In 1976, at the invitation of the President of Mexico, we opened a house in that nation. Our sisters, as is the custom in our congregation, were full of activity—seeing everyone, walking tirelessly until their legs could endure no more, trying to discover where the greatest need was in order to begin there.

They found deep poverty everywhere in Mexico. All the zones they visited appeared immensely poor. But no one asked them for clothing or medicine or food—nothing. Only, "Teach us the Word of God."

I was very surprised. Those people are hungry for God: "Teach us the Word of God."

• I believe that we should realize that poverty doesn't only consist in being hungry for bread, but rather it is a tremendous hunger for human dignity. We need to love and to be somebody for someone else. This is where we make our mistake and shove people aside. Not only have we denied the poor a piece of bread, but by thinking that they have no worth and leaving them abandoned in the streets, we have denied them the human dignity that is rightfully theirs as children of God. They are my brothers and sisters as long as they are there. And why am I not in their place? This should be a very important question. We could have been in their place if we had not received the love and affection that has been given to us.

• I am deeply impressed by the fact that before explaining the Word of God, before presenting to the crowds the eight beatitudes, Jesus had compassion on them and gave them food. Only then did he begin to teach them.

# FIFTEEN

## *You Did It for Me*

Here we come to the heart of Mother Teresa's prayer and work: "Whatever you did for one of these least brothers of mine, you did for me" (see Matthew 25:40). When Mother Teresa looks into the face of a dying, worm-eaten, homeless man, she sees Jesus. When she bathes his body, she anoints Jesus for burial. When she puts her arms around him, she worships Jesus.

This vision of Jesus in suffering human beings is what makes Mother Teresa a missionary and not a social worker. It is what transforms her work from a thankless, menial task to a work of devotion. It is what makes her light shine so that the world, seeing her work, gives glory to the Father in heaven.

*Come, O blessed of my Father,*
*inherit the kingdom prepared for you*
*from the foundation of the world;*
*for I was hungry and you gave me food,*
*I was thirsty and you gave me drink,*
*I was a stranger and you welcomed me,*
*I was naked and you clothed me,*
*I was sick and you visited me,*
*I was in prison and you came to me....*
*As you did it to one of the least of these my brethren,*
*you did it to me.*

Matthew 25:34-36,40, RSV

*Come, O blessed of my Father,*
*inherit the kingdom prepared for you*
*from the foundation of the world...*

• We all long for heaven where God is, but we have it in our power to be in heaven with him right now—to be happy with him at this very moment. But being happy with him now means loving like he loves, helping like he helps, giving as he gives, serving as he serves, rescuing as he rescues, being with him twenty-four hours a day—touching him in his distressing disguise.

• Our Savior's poverty is greater even than that of the poorest of the world's beasts. "The foxes have holes and birds of the air their nests but the Son of Man has nowhere to lay his head" (see Luke 9:58). So it was in fact. He had no house of his own, no fixed abode. The Samaritans had just turned him away and he must seek for shelter. Everything was uncertain: lodging and food. He received whatever he used as alms from the charity of others.

Such is indeed great poverty—how touching it is when we think who he is, the God-Man, the Lord of heaven and earth, and what he might have possessed! But it is this which makes his poverty majestic and rich, that it is a voluntary poverty chosen out of love for us and with the intention of enriching us.

We are blessed in being called to share in our own little way the great poverty of this great God. We are thrilled also at the magnificent vagabondage of our life. We do not roam, but we cultivate the vagabond spirit of abandonment. We have nothing to live on, yet we live splendidly; nothing to walk on, yet we walk fearlessly; nothing to lean on, but yet we lean on God confidently; for we are his own and he is our provident Father.

• In order to help us deserve heaven, Christ set a condition: that at the moment of our death you and I—whoever we might have been and wherever we have lived, Christians and non-Christians alike, every human being who has been created by the loving hand of God in his own image—shall stand in his presence and be judged according to what we have been for the poor, what we have done for them.

Here a beautiful standard for judgment presents itself. We have to become increasingly aware that the poor are the hope of humanity, for we will be judged by how we have treated the poor. We will have to face this reality when we are summoned before the throne of God: "I was hungry. I was naked. I was homeless. And whatever you did to the least of my brethren, you did it to me."

• Jesus says, "Whatever you do to the least of your brothers is in my name. When you receive a little child you receive me. If in my name you give a glass of water, you give it to me." And to make sure that we understand what he is talking about, he says that at the hour of death we are going to be judged only that way. I was hungry, you gave me to eat. I was naked, you clothed me. I was homeless, you took me in. Hunger is not only for bread; hunger is for love. Nakedness is not only for a piece of clothing; nakedness is lack of human dignity, and also that beautiful virtue of purity, and lack of that respect for each other. Homelessness is not only being without a home made of bricks; homelessness is also being rejected, unwanted, unloved.

*... for I was hungry and you gave me food,*
*I was thirsty and you gave me drink,*
*I was a stranger and you welcomed me,*
*I was naked and you clothed me,*
*I was sick and you visited me,*
*I was in prison and you came to me...*

• A sister was telling me that just two or three weeks ago she and some other sisters picked up a man from the streets in Bombay and brought him home. We have a big place donated to us which we have turned into a home for the dying. This man was brought there and the sisters took care of him. They loved him and treated him with dignity. Right away they discovered that the whole of his back had no skin, no flesh. It was all eaten up. After they washed him they put him on his bed, and this sister told me that she had never seen so much joy as she saw on the face of that man. Then I asked her, "What did you feel when you were removing those worms from his body; what did you feel?" And she looked at me and said, "I've never felt the presence of Christ; I've never really believed the word of Jesus saying, 'I was sick and you did it to me.' But his presence was there and I could see it on that man's face." This is the gift of God.

• The fullness of our heart comes in our actions: how I treat that leper, how I treat that dying person, how I treat the homeless. Sometimes it is more difficult to work with the street people than with the people in our homes for the dying because the dying are peaceful and waiting; they are ready to go to God. You can touch the sick and believe, or you can touch the leper and believe, that it is the body of Christ you are touching, but it is much more difficult when these people are drunk or shouting to think that this is Jesus in that distressing disguise. How clean and loving our hands must be to be able to bring that compassion to them!

• How pure our hands ought to be if we are to touch the body of Christ, just as the priest touches it under the likeness of bread. With what veneration and love does he lift up the consecrated Host! The same should our feeling be every time we touch the body of a sick person.

It was this insight that transformed Father Damien into an apostle to the lepers, that made St. Vincent de Paul the father of the poor. St. Peter Claver used to lick the wounds of the black slaves. St. Francis of Assisi too, when he met a completely disfigured leper, at first wanted to run away but then embraced that horrible face. And this action filled him with unspeakable joy, to the point that the leper went away thanking God for his healing.

Why all this? Because all of these saints wanted to get as close as possible to God's own heart.

• Hungry for love, he looks at you.
Thirsty for kindness, he begs from you.

Naked for loyalty, he hopes in you.
Sick and imprisoned for friendship, he wants from you.
Homeless for shelter in your heart, he asks of you.
Will you be that one to him?

• Christ said, "I was hungry and you gave me food." He was hungry not only for bread but for the understanding love of being loved, of being known, of being someone to someone. He was naked not only of clothing but of human dignity and of respect, through the injustice that is done to the poor, who are looked down upon simply because they are poor. He was dispossessed not only of a house made of bricks but because of the dispossession of those who are locked up, of those who are unwanted and unloved, of those who walk through the world with no one to care for them.

• We give immediate and effective service to the poorest of the poor, as long as they have no one to help them, by—

- —feeding the hungry: not only with food but also with the Word of God;
- —giving drink to the thirsty: not only for water, but for knowledge, peace, truth, justice, and love;
- —clothing the naked: not only with clothes, but also with human dignity;
- —giving shelter to the homeless: not only a shelter made of bricks, but a heart that understands, that covers, that loves;
- —nursing the sick and the dying: not only the body, but also the mind and spirit.

• Nakedness is not only the need for a piece of clothing. Nakedness is the need for human dignity which people sometimes lose, which we unjustly take away from the poor. We think they are useless and hopeless. We have so many adjectives for poor people! That is the real nakedness of our world today. Nakedness is being thrown away by society, unwanted, deserted. That man, that woman, that child—it does not matter who—is unwanted and thrown away.

• Our works of love are nothing but works of peace. Let us do them with greater love and efficiency, each one in her own or his own work in daily life; in your home, in your neighborhood, it is always the same Christ who says:

I was hungry: not only for food but for peace that comes from a pure heart.

I was thirsty: not for water but for peace that satiates the passionate thirst of passion for war.

I was naked: not for clothes, but for that beautiful dignity of men and women for their bodies.

I was homeless: not for a shelter made of bricks but for a heart that understands, that covers, that loves.

• During the passion, Jesus' face was like the face of a leper. When I see lepers I think that the passion of Christ is being re-lived in them. They are wonderful. They have no bitterness in their lives. At this very moment we are caring for fifty-three thousand lepers in India. It is wonderful to see how these people want to go on living. We are building rehabilitation centers. They have their own dispensaries and schools. They do their own work, and they lead a normal life. This has brought a new life and a new joy to their old lives. This also makes them feel like beloved children of God.

*As you did it to one of the least of these*
*my brethren, you did it to me.*

• When we handle the sick and the needy we touch the suffering body of Christ and this touch will make us heroic; it will make us forget the repugnance and the natural tendencies in us. We need the eyes of deep faith to see Christ in the broken body and dirty clothes under which the most beautiful one among the sons of men hides. We shall need the hands of Christ to touch these bodies wounded by pain and suffering.

• We need to be pure in heart to see Jesus in the person of the spiritually poorest. Therefore the more disfigured the image of God is in that person, the greater will be our faith and devotion in seeking Jesus' face and lovingly ministering to him. We consider it an honor to serve Christ in the distressing disguise of the spiritually poorest; we do it with deep gratitude and reverence in a spirit of fraternal sharing.

• Whatever you do, even if you help somebody cross the road, you do it to Jesus. Even giving somebody a glass of water, you do it to Jesus. Such simple little teaching, but it is more and more important.

• The greatness of our vocation lies also in the fact that we are called upon to minister to Christ himself in the distressing disguise of the poor and suffering. We are called upon every day to exercise our priestly ministry of handling the body of Christ in the form of a suffering humanity and of giving Holy Communion to all those with whom we come in contact by spreading the fragrance of his love wherever we go.

• I know you all love the poor—otherwise you would not join—but let each one of us try to make this love more kind, more charitable, more cheerful. Let our eyes see more clearly in deep faith the face of Christ in the face of the poor.

• In the poor, and in our sisters and brothers, it is Jesus, and so we are twenty-four hours in his presence. Therefore we are contemplatives in the heart of the world. If we would only learn how to pray the work by doing it with Jesus, for Jesus, to Jesus, for the glory of his name and the good of souls!

• May we never forget that in the service to the poor we are offered a magnificent opportunity to do something beautiful for God. In fact, when we give ourselves with all our hearts to the poor, it is Christ whom we are serving in their disfigured faces. For he himself said, "You did it to me."

• If we really understand the Eucharist, if we really center our lives on Jesus' body and blood, if we nourish our lives with the bread of the Eucharist, it will be easy for us to see Christ in that hungry one next door, the one lying in the gutter, that alcoholic man we shun, our husband or our wife, or our restless child. For in them, we will recognize the distressing disguises of the poor: Jesus in our midst.

• Each time you make these sacrifices, each time you think of the poor both near and far off, every time you give up something you would like and give it to the poor, you are feeding the hungry Christ, you are clothing the naked Christ, you are giving a home to the homeless Christ. Whether you are directly serving the poor or not, whenever you think of the poor and make sacrifices for them, you are really doing it to Christ.

• If everyone were capable of discovering the image of God in their neighbors, do you think that we would still need tanks and generals?

**Q:** *When will the day come in which the sea of poverty disappears?*
**MT:** When all of us recognize that our suffering neighbor is the image of God himself and when we understand the consequences of that truth. That day poverty will no longer exist and we, the Missionaries of Charity, will no longer have any work to do.

• You may go out into the street and have nothing to say—all right, but maybe there is a man standing there on the corner and you go to him. Maybe he resents you, but you are there, and that presence is there. You must radiate that presence that is within you, in the way you address that man with love and respect. Why? Because you believe that is Jesus. Jesus cannot receive you: for this you must know how to go to him. He comes disguised in the form of that person there.

• You cannot have the vow of charity if you have not got the faith to see Jesus in the people you meet. Otherwise our work is no more than social work. What if you feel a disgust and run away? Feelings don't count. Run away but come back without delay.

• On one occasion when we were discussing food supplies and other such things, a senator from the United States said, "Turning our backs on the poor is the same as turning our backs on Christ." You can apply this truth to yourself. If you truly strive to give your whole lives to Christ and try to help people to see Christ in others, if you love Christ in your neighbor and love one another as Christ loves you, you will understand.

• It is the individual that is important to us. In order to love a person, one must come close to him or her. If we wait until there is a given number of people, we will get lost in numbers and will never be able to show respect and love for one concrete person. To me, every person in the world is unique.

# SIXTEEN

## *Let the Children Come to Me*

Mother Teresa is not a romantic. She has seen death in all its ugliness, and she has no illusions about it. She knows that abortion is a particularly heinous kind of death. An aborted child cannot die at peace, with dignity, surrounded by love. It is a victim of violence, the most unwanted of all human beings.

For Mother Teresa, the large number of abortions in the United States and many other developed countries is intolerable. She has no fear of telling presidents and prime ministers that their abortion policies are wrong. And she definitively answers all those who charge that people who are pro-life do not care about the children after they are born. "Please don't destroy any child," she pleads with government officials. "I will take any child, any time, night or day. Just let me know and I will come for him."

Not only does she sponsor children's homes and homes for unwed mothers, she also has been instrumental in a large number of adoption placements. This chapter shows how deeply Mother Teresa cares for children, born and unborn.

*Then children were brought to him*
*that he might lay his hands on them and pray.*
*The disciples rebuked the people; but Jesus said,*
*"Let the children come to me,*
*and do not hinder them;*
*for to such belongs the kingdom of heaven."*

Matthew 19:13-14, RSV

• In the slums the sisters find a place where they will gather the little street children, whoever they may be. Their first concern is to make them clean, feed them, and only then teach them, just a little reading and writing. Religion must be proposed to them in a simple, interesting, and attractive way. Whatever the sisters teach, first there must always be something the children can enjoy and yet at the same time learn.

• Let the sisters bring the children to Mass. Do your best to get them. If you have to run for a child, do it and God in his infinite mercy may give the light and grace to that soul because of all the trouble you took. Never lose sight of the mercy of God. Take the trouble to help the children to love the Mass, to know the meaning of the Mass, to join in the Mass through simple prayers and hymns. Be careful of the attitude you take while minding the children during Mass. Do not correct loudly. Keep your hands joined. Join in the prayers and the singing. The children will do exactly what you do.

• All over the world, terrible suffering, terrible hunger for love. So bring prayer in your family, bring it to your little children. Teach them to pray. For a child that prays is a happy child. A family that prays is a united family. We hear of so many broken families. And then we examine them: why are they broken? I think because they never pray together. They are never one in prayer before the Lord.

• When visiting the families you will meet with very much misery. Sometimes you will find a little child watching near a dying parent, or holding the head of a dead parent. It is then that you must put out all your energy to help that little child in his sorrow. Once there were found two little children near the dead body of their father, who had died two days before. Thank God, sisters came and rescued the children and got a proper burial for the father.

• Again and again we hear that sentence, "Unless you become like a little child, you cannot enter into heaven" (see Matthew 18:4 and Luke 18:17). And what is being a little child? It is having a clean heart, a pure heart, a heart that holds Jesus, a heart that can say again and again, "Jesus in my heart, I believe in your tender love for me. I love you." This is the heart that you, and I, even the youngest, must have to be able to look up, to look up at the cross and understand how much Jesus loved me, loved each one of us separately.

• We are here to be witnesses of love and to celebrate life, because life has been created in the image of God. Life is to love and to be loved.

That is why we all have to take a strong stand so that no child—boy or girl—will be rejected or unloved. Every child is a sign of God's love, that has to be extended over all the earth.

If you hear of someone who does not want to have her child, who wants to have an abortion, try to convince her to bring the child to me. I will love that child, who is a sign of God's love.

• An incredible poverty exists today. Unborn children are aborted because they are unwanted. Children die in their mother's wombs because they are unwanted. A nation that allows abortion is a very poor one. A mother who is capable of killing her own child only because she is afraid of having another one is poor indeed! She is afraid of feeding one more child and educating one more child. She prefers to have another television set or an automobile instead. A child condemned to death for that! Nevertheless, we read in Scripture: "Even if a mother should forsake her child, I will not forsake you. I have you in the palm of my hand" (see Isaiah 49:15-16).

• If a mother can kill her own child, how long will it be before we start to kill one another? We should not be surprised when we hear about murders, deaths, wars, and hate in the world today. Don't ever allow even one child, born or unborn, to be unwanted. Let's go with Our Lady to search out that child and take him or her home.

• We, the Missionaries of Charity, have homes for the sick and dying in many places. We also have children's homes for the unwanted, the unloved, the sick, and the retarded.

God has been just wonderful to us by giving us more parents, especially in India, who want to adopt our children. We have many children ready to be adopted.

People very often make jokes with me (or about me, rather), because we are also teaching natural family planning. They say, "Mother Teresa is doing plenty of talking about family planning, but she herself does not practice it. She is having more and more children every day."

Indeed, that is the way it is. Our homes are always full of children. And as they come, God has been tremendously wonderful to us.... You would be surprised how much love is showered on those unwanted little children, who otherwise would have been destined to live in the gutter.

Lately, I have experienced what a child meant for the family that adopted him. I had given the child to a high-class family. After some time, I heard that the child was sick and completely crippled.

So I sent to the family and said, "Give the child back to me and I will give you a healthy one!"

The father said to me, "Take my life first, before you take this child!"

That shows you what the child meant to that family and how beautifully that little one, in spite of all his suffering, had fit into the lives of those people. These are some of the great things that God is doing with us and through us, with your help.

• I am very happy to be surrounded by children, because Jesus had a very special love for children. Many children came to see Jesus, and the apostles said to them, "Don't come!" But Jesus said, "Let the children come to me. I love them."

• I cannot remember now in what city I was, but I do remember that I did not see any children on the street. I missed the children very badly. While I was walking down the street, suddenly I saw a baby carriage. A young woman was pushing the carriage, and I crossed the street just to see the child.

To my terrible surprise, there was no child in the carriage. There was a little dog!

Apparently the hunger in the heart of that woman had to be satisfied. So, not having a child, she looked for a substitute. She found a dog. In many places, children are neglected, but animals are cared for and pampered. Animals are given special food and special things.

I love dogs myself very much, but still I cannot bear seeing a dog given the place of a child.

• We have many children in our homes for unwed mothers; one hundred seventy babies are born every day. Can you imagine that? Yet God has worked a miracle. Even in India, every day we have one or two families who come to adopt a child. Many come from abroad, but many children are being adopted in India.

You may not understand this great miracle, but for us who live in India, who work among Indians, this is the greatest miracle that could happen. According to the caste system, my children and myself and all the sisters are untouchables. Therefore, to take one of our children into a family is something unbelievable. It goes against the whole cultural and religious life of the nation. Nevertheless, Indian parents are really taking our children in.

I remember when I told Mrs. Indira Gandhi, the former prime minister of India, what I was doing with the children. She said, "No, that is not possible!"

I said to her, "But we are doing it. It must be possible!"

• Our children may be only slum children, but for that very reason "just anything" will not do. Each sister must find a way to attract, to capture the hearts of the children.

Don't think that you need not prepare the lessons because you know more than they. They must have the best, and their good must be uppermost in your mind. Don't get stale in your methods, like stagnant water. Keep on improving yourself. Try new ways and means. You may have the knowledge, but you must also know how to impart it.

Our children come to school with empty stomachs—don't waste their time. They must learn something—to be able to read and write a little and tell a little about the life of our Lord. Make them happy.

They have had much to suffer already, and we cannot treat them as we would children going to a regular school.

• Our children, we want them, we love them; but what of the other millions? Many people are very, very concerned with the children of India, with the children of Africa, where quite a number die of malnutrition, of hunger, and so on. But millions of others are dying by the will of their own mothers. And this is what is the greatest destroyer of peace today. Because if a mother can kill her own child, what is left before I kill you and you kill me? There is nothing in between.

• A nation that destroys the life of an unborn child, who has been created for living and loving, who has been created in the image of God, is in a tremendous poverty. For a child to be destroyed because of the selfishness of those who fear they may not be able to feed one more child, fear they may not be able to educate one more child, and so decide that the child has to die—that's poverty.

• There are so many children today who are categorized as undesired, as unwanted. The problem that worries so many people is that the world is beginning to look too populated. What concerns my sisters and me is that people do not think that divine providence can provide for the new ones, for the unborn.

In my opinion, if abortion is allowed in the rich countries, who possess all that money can provide, then those are the poorest among the poor. I would like to open in such countries many houses for children, in order to welcome them and provide what they need. We have many such houses in all of India, and up to now we have never seen the need to reject any child.

The most wonderful thing is that each child who has escaped death by the hands of his parents has later found a home with new parents. For some years now in Calcutta we have been trying to prevent abortions by means of adoptions. Thanks to God, we have been able to offer many who otherwise would have died, a father and a mother to love them and to offer them affection and care.

• I think that the cry of children who are assassinated before they come into the world is surely heard by God.

Jesus has said that we are much more important in the eyes of his Father than the grass, the birds, or the lilies of the field. He has also said that if the Father cares for all these things, much more will he care for his own life in us.

Jesus cannot deceive us. Life is the greatest gift of God to human beings, and man has been created in the image of God. Life belongs to God, and we have no right to destroy it.

• We must pray for those countries that have passed laws that accept abortion as a natural action. This is a transgression! Their sin is great.

When we were invited to take care of the young women of Bangladesh who had been raped by soldiers, we saw the need to open a home for children. The difficulties were great because accepting in society young women who had been raped went against both Hindu and Muslim laws. But when the leader of Bangladesh said that those young women were heroines of the nation—who had fought for their own purity, who had struggled for their country—their very parents came to look for them. In many cases we were able to find young men who offered to marry them.

Some people favored abortion. It was a terrible struggle, if I can say it that way, that we had to fight with them. I told them that the young women had been violated, that they did not want to sin; whereas now what the men wanted to do was to force them or to help them to commit a transgression that would accompany them throughout their lives. I told them that these mothers would never forget that they had killed their own children.

Thanks be to God, the government accepted our conditions. The people were told that each of the children for whom abortion would have been chosen should be taken to the house of Mother Teresa to receive help. Of the forty children we received, more than thirty went to Canada and other countries, adopted by generous families.

• I have been told in more than one place, "If you have to give birth to a child, you have to pay so much. And if you have an abortion, you won't have to pay anything."

My sisters and I, we want to save that child. We will help that woman to bring her pregnancy to term and give birth to that child. We will pay whatever it costs. We will make the necessary sacrifices in order to pay.

I have sent word to all the police stations, clinics, and hospitals, "Please don't destroy any child. I will take any child, any time, night or day. Just let me know and I will come for him." Our homes for children are overflowing.

And what a wonderful gift of God is seen when a child is loved and cared for! God's blessing is evident in such beautiful work. It is so beautiful that we have many families that adopt these children we care for. So we are bringing joy into the homes of those who have no children, who cannot have children. We are giving a father's and a mother's love to a child who would have been destroyed.

See the wonderful ways of God! This is really love in action!

• Let us stop for a moment to pray for our parents, for having loved and wanted us, for having given us life.

In the Gospels we read that God so loved the world that he gave us Jesus through the most pure Virgin. As soon as she received the announcement from the angel, Mary went in haste to her cousin Elizabeth, who was with child. And the unborn child John the Baptist rejoiced in Elizabeth's womb. How wonderful it was—Almighty God chose an unborn child to announce the coming of his Son!

Yet today, unborn children are targeted for death, persons to be discarded and destroyed. Abortion destroys the image of God. It is the most terrible plague in our society, the greatest killer of love and peace. Those little children still unborn have been created for bigger things: to love and to be loved.

• A child is the greatest of God's gifts to a family, because it is the fruit of the parents' love.

• The other day I was talking to a woman who had had an abortion eight years ago. What do you think she told me?

"Mother, I feel a pain in my heart whenever I see a child. When I see a child who is eight years old, I always think of my child who would be eight years old. It is an awful pang in my heart, believe me."

She was a Hindu, with a different degree of sensitivity to the value of human life, but Christian or non-Christian, that mother's love, that mother's pain, is there. Right up to the end of her life she will know, "I have killed my child, I decided to have my child destroyed!"

What can we do? If necessary, let us start homes where we can gather together these children. Maybe they are not wanted, or maybe their parents cannot afford to take care of them. Let us then decide to take care of them ourselves.

By doing so, you and I will do something beautiful for God. We will give a wonderful home to children who would otherwise be destroyed and unwanted. We will fill those mothers' hearts with joy. Because, deep down in their hearts, they feel so sad.

• I must tell you something that was a surprise for me and may be a surprise for you.

We deal with thousands and thousands of very poor people in Calcutta. As you may know, there are over ten million people in that city, but up to now I am not aware of one woman among the very poor who has had an abortion.

All of them have given birth to their children.

At times they might put their children in the garbage, hoping that someone will take care of them. But I know of not one who has decided to destroy her child.

• People are trying to be free to live their own life by destroying life. For me, this is a painful sign that either the country is so poor that it cannot care for the lives that God has created, or that people are making a tremendous mistake.

I don't want to talk about what should be legal or illegal. I don't think that any human heart should dare to take life, or any human hand be raised to destroy life. Life is the life of God in us. The life of

God is present even in the fetus. We don't have even the slightest right to destroy a life, whether it is that of a child, a man, or a woman. It's all the same. I believe that the cry of these children, these ones who are never born because they are killed before they ever saw the light of day, must offend God greatly.

Jesus said that we are much more important to his Father than the grass in the field, the sparrows, or the lilies of the field. If he takes care of things such as these, which are only things, how much more would he care for our lives!

He will not deceive us. Life is the greatest gift that God has bestowed on human beings. Since human life is created in the image of God, it belongs to him. We have no right to destroy it.

• God has invested all his love in creating that human life. That is why we are not entitled to destroy it, especially we who know that Christ has died for the salvation of that life. Christ has died and has given everything for that child.

• Our sisters work in the slums. There we frequently run across young mothers who are about to die and children with deformities. Through research we discovered that men have abused these young women, taking advantage of their ignorance.

We began to ask God to send us someone to take care of this work, to help such women cope with this difficulty with a clear conscience, a healthy body, and in a happy family. There came to us a sister from Mauritius Island who had attended a course on family planning.

We started with an information program. Right now there are more than three thousand families who use natural family planning, and it has been about 95 percent effective. When people see these good effects in their families, they come to us to say thanks. Some of them have said, "Our family has stayed together, in good health, and we can have a child when we desire it."

• It is true, people are very anxious about the future and about overpopulation. But there is natural family planning. That method can help couples plan their family without destroying God's gift of life.

I think we should train our children for the future by teaching them to respect the dignity of life, by teaching them that life is a gift from God, something created by him, something to be lived for him. By the purity and sanctity of their lives, they will then be able to face the future using simple, natural means that God has created.

By properly using the natural family planning method, couples are using their bodies to glorify God in the sanctity of family life. I think that if we could bring this method to every country, if our poor people would learn it, there would be more peace, more love in the family between parents and children.

• We are carrying out something else that is very beautiful. We are teaching natural family planning to our beggars, our lepers, our slum dwellers, and our homeless street people. The method we teach them is very beautiful and simple. Our poor understand it. I believe that if our people can do this, how much more can all the rest of us! We can use the means of natural family planning and decide not to destroy the life that God has created in us!

• I think the world today is upside-down. It is suffering so much because there is so little love in the home and in family life.

We have no time for our children.

We have no time for each other.

There is no time to enjoy each other.

Love lives in homes, and the lack of love causes so much suffering and unhappiness in the world today.

Everybody today seems to be in such a terrible rush, anxious for greater development and greater riches, so that children have very little time for their parents. And parents have very little time for their children and for each other.

So the breakdown of peace in the world begins at home.

People who really and truly love each other are the happiest people in the world. We see that with our very poor people. They love their children and they love their families. They may have very little, in fact, they may not have anything, but they are happy people.

• If we help our children to be what they should be today, then, when tomorrow becomes today, they will have the necessary courage to face it with greater love.

Right from the very beginning, since love begins at home, I think we should teach our children to love one another at home. They can learn this only from their father and mother, when they see the parents' love for each other.

I think this will strengthen our children, so that they can give that love to others in the future.

• People are afraid of having children.

Children have lost their place in the family.

Children are very lonely, very lonely!

When children come home from school, there is no one to greet them. Then they go back to the streets.

We must find our children again and bring them back home.

Mothers are at the heart of the family. Children need their mothers. If the mother is there, the children will be there too. For the family to be whole, the children and the mother also need the father to be present in the home.

I think if we can help to bring them all back together, we will do a beautiful thing for God.

• If in your family, your young daughter or son has done something wrong, forgive them. Show them the forgiving heart of God.

• If we have trouble in families today, it is because children are lost. It is necessary for us to pray and then, with Our Lady, go out and look for the children to bring them home.

• Jesus was born into a family and stayed in Nazareth for thirty years. He had come to redeem the world, yet he spent thirty years in Nazareth, doing the humble work of an ordinary person. He spent all those years just living out family life.

• One day I found a little girl in the street, so I took her to our children's home. We have a nice place and good food there. We gave her clean clothes and we made her as happy as we could.

After a few hours, the little girl ran away. I looked for her, but I couldn't find her anywhere. Then after a few days, I found her again.

And, again, I brought her to our home and told a sister, "Sister, please, follow this child wherever she goes."

The little girl ran away again. But the sister followed to find out where she was going and why she kept running away.

She followed the little girl and discovered that the little one's mother was living under a tree in the street. The mother had placed two stones there and did her cooking under that tree.

The sister sent word to me and I went there. I found joy on that little girl's face, because she was with her mother who loved her and was making special food for her in that little open place.

I asked the little girl, "How is it that you would not stay with us? You had so many beautiful things in our home."

She answered, "I could not live without my mother. She loves me." That little girl was happier to have the meager food her mother was cooking in the street than all the things I had given her.

While the child was with us, I could scarcely see a smile on her face. But when I found her there with her mother, in the street, they were smiling.

Why?

Because they were family.

• I have another conviction that I want to share with you. Love begins at home, and every Co-worker should try to make sure that deep family love abides in his or her home. Only when love abides at home can we share it with our next-door neighbor. Then it will show forth and you will be able to say to them, "Yes, love is here." And then you will be able to share it with everyone around you.

• Perhaps in our own families, there is someone who feels lonely, who is sick, or who is overburdened with worry. Are we there, open and willing to offer support and affection? Are you, mothers, available to your children?

I was surprised to find out how many young people in the slums, both boys and girls, are involved with drugs. I have tried to find out why. "Why is this happening?" I asked.

The answer was, "There is no one at home to love them. Parents are too busy and don't have time for them. Young parents are so involved in social commitments and activities that their children go out into the streets and get mixed up in something which is bad for them." Here we are talking about peace, and these are the very things that shatter peace.

•The work that each one of you carries out in your families for those you love is an expression of your love for God. Love starts at home. For your love to be real, it cannot waver at home.

# SEVENTEEN

# *Love One Another, As I Have Loved You*

The word *love* permeates Mother Teresa's speaking. Jesus commands us to love one another. This love is to be based on his love for us. We love God, who loves the world. Through us, the world learns of God's love.

The kind of love that counts is a sacrificial love. It isn't enough just to give from our abundance. We must give, we must love, until it hurts. Jesus loved us so much that he endured betrayal, false accusations, torture, ridicule, physical pain, and finally death. As followers of Jesus, we too must be willing to suffer for others.

Love begins at home with those closest to us. If we don't love our family members—our spouse, our children, our aging parents, the brothers or sisters in our religious order—how can we reach out with God's love to the world?

People everywhere are hungry for God's love. We must radiate that love. When we do, then they will know that we are followers of Jesus. Then God can use us to fill people's hunger for him.

*A new commandment I give to you,*
*that you love one another;*
*even as I have loved you,*
*that you also love one another.*
*By this all men will know that you are my disciples,*
*if you have love for one another.*

**John 13:34-35, RSV**

*A new commandment I give you,*
*that you love one another...*

- Love has a hem to her garment
  That reaches the very dust.
  It sweeps the stains
  From the streets and lanes,
  And because it can, it must.

• Be kind and loving with each other, for you cannot love Christ in his distressing disguise if you cannot love Jesus in the heart of your brothers and sisters. Love, to be living, must be fed on sacrifice. Be generous with the penances and all the sacrifices that come from our poverty, and you will be able in all sincerity to say, "My God and my all."

• You are to be a family, to be that presence of Christ to each other. Love each other tenderly as Jesus loves each one of you. That is the holiness of the Universal Brothers of the Word: tender love for each other speaks much louder than all the words you can say. Never hurt anybody with the Word, which is so sacred in our lives. Really live what you say: the younger brothers that come up learn by seeing, not so much by hearing. Young people now don't want to listen; they want to see.

• A few weeks ago I got a letter from a little child from the United States. She was making her first Holy Communion. She told her parents, "Don't worry about special clothes for my First Communion. I will make my First Communion in my school uniform. Don't have any party for me. But please give me the money. I want to send it to Mother Teresa." That little one, just seven or eight years old, already in her heart was loving until it hurt.

• Hear Jesus your Co-worker speak to you: "I want you to be my fire of love amongst the poor, the sick, the dying, and the little children; the poor I want you to bring to me." Learn this sentence by heart and when you are wanting in generosity, repeat it. We can refuse Christ just as we refuse others: "I will not give you my hands to work with, my feet to walk with, my mind to study with, my heart to love with. You knock at the door, but I will not give you the key of my heart." This is what he feels so bitterly: not being able to live his life in a soul.

• The Indian ambassador in Rome told the people, "These our sisters have done more in a short time to bring our two countries closer to each other by their influence of love than we have through official means."

• If you don't have love for one another, then how can you love Christ? How can they see Jesus in you? That's why we need a clean heart, to see Jesus. Love one another. That's all Jesus came to teach us. The whole gospel is very, very simple. Do you love me? Obey my commandments. He's turning and twisting just to get around to one thing: love one another. He wants us to be really, really loving. Give from the heart.

• Intense love does not measure; it just gives. To be an apostle of the Sacred Heart, one must be burning with love, intense love for the sisters. If you want peace, you cannot just say anything you please, the first word that comes into your head.

• We desire to be able to welcome Jesus at Christmas time, not in a cold manger of our heart but in a heart full of love and humility, in a heart so pure, so immaculate, so warm with love for one another.

• Do not pursue spectacular deeds. What matters is the gift of your self, the degree of love that you put into each one of your actions.

• We need no bombs or weapons. Love is our weapon: love toward the lepers, the elderly, the dying, the paralytic; toward all those who have no one and are loved by no one.

• Love is a fruit in season and out of season, without limits—a fruit that is available to all.

• Not even God can fill what is already full. Hence we have to empty our hearts in order to allow him to fill us with his love and with his kindness.

• I cannot forget my mother. She was usually very busy all day long. But when sunset drew near, it was her custom to hurry with her tasks in order to be ready to receive my father.

At the time we did not understand, and we would smile and even joke a little about it. Today I cannot help but call to mind that great delicacy of love that she had for him. No matter what happened, she was always prepared, with a smile on her lips, to welcome him.

Today we have no time. Fathers and mothers are so busy that when children come home they are not welcomed with love or with a smile.

• "Love one another." Suppress this command, and the whole work of the Church of Christ will fall.

Charity toward the poor must be a burning flame in our Society. Just as the fire, when it ceases burning, spreads no more warmth, so the Missionaries of Charity, should they lack love, would lose all usefulness and would have no more life.

Charity is like a living flame: the drier the fuel, the livelier the flame. Likewise our hearts, when they are free of all earthly causes, commit themselves in free service.

Love of God must give rise to a total service. The more disgusting the work, the greater must love be, as it takes succor to the Lord disguised in the rags of the poor.

• I always say—and I don't get tired of repeating it—that love starts at home. I will never forget that I was in a country once where there were many Co-workers, but two of the coordinators for the Co-workers were very distant from each other. And they were husband and wife. They came to me and I told them, "I can't understand how you are able to give Jesus to others if you can't give him to each other. How can you find Jesus hidden under the distressing appearance of the poor if you cannot see him in each other?"

The husband and wife started up an endless argument. Both of them let out all their frustrations and hurts, saying everything they had to say. Then I interrupted. "Now that's enough. You have said everything that you needed to say. Let's go to Jesus so that you can tell him all these things."

We went to the chapel and the two knelt down before the altar. After a few moments, the husband turned to his wife and said, "You are my only love in this world, the only one I love and have." Other things of that sort followed. It was all very beautiful.

Now all the Co-workers there have changed for the better. Why? Because those in charge of the group have come to understand that if we don't accept Jesus in one another, we will not be able to give him to others.

• Sometimes we see how joy returns to the lives of the most destitute when they realize that many among us are concerned about them and show them our love. Even their health improves if they are sick.

• If my love for my sisters is okay, then my love for Jesus will be okay. There are not two loves. The deeper my love for Jesus, the deeper that love for my sisters, the greater the zeal to go to the poor.

• Charity, to be fruitful, must cost us. Actually, we hear so much about charity. Yet we never give it its full importance: God put the commandment of loving our neighbor on the same footing as the first commandment. God's love is infinite.

God has prepared us for service, so he expects this from us. He has given each of us something that in one way or another will enable him to shine through us.

We want to be something for Almighty God, and since we cannot reach God and do it directly to him, we serve him in the poor people of India. We are here purely for the love of God. Our charity must be true. We must feel in our very bones that we are doing it—we should be living fires of love. Every Missionary of Charity must be like a burning bush.

• If we learn the art of recollection, we will look more and more like Christ since his heart is nothing but reward: Christ always thinks about others.

Jesus walked among men doing only good. At Cana Mary did nothing but think about the needs of others and let Jesus know about them.

The recollection of Jesus, Mary, and Joseph was so deep that they changed Nazareth into the dwelling of the Almighty. If we too could have that same concern for one another, our communities would also become the dwelling places of the Almighty.

• Use your tongue for the good of others—for out of the abundance of the heart the mouth speaks.

• Since we cannot see Christ, we cannot express our love to him. But we do see our neighbor, and we can do for him what we would do for Christ if he were visible.

Let us be open to God, so that he can use us. Let us put love into action.

Let us begin with our family, with our closest neighbors. It is difficult, but that is where our work begins. We are collaborators of Christ, fertile branches on the vine.

• In order for love to be genuine, it has to be above all a love for my neighbor.

• We must love those who are nearest to us, in our own family. From there, love spreads toward whomever may need us.

• We must try to discover the poor in our own setting because only if we know them will we be able to understand them and to offer them our love. And only when we love them will we be willing to offer them our service of love.

• It is easy to love those who live far away. It is not always easy to love those who live right next to us. It is easier to offer a dish of rice to meet the hunger of a needy person than to comfort the loneliness and the anguish of someone in our own home who does not feel loved.

• There are young people who come from all over the world to spend two weeks or a month working at the humblest of jobs out of love for others. They pick up all sorts of people off the streets for us, but they do it with a great deal of love. I feel unable to explain adequately what happens to those who lovingly serve the poor and what also happens to the people who are lovingly served. These homes of ours have become homes in which treasures of the kingdom are hidden.

*... Even as I have loved you,*
*that you also love one another.*

• These words of Jesus, "Even as I have loved you that you also love one another," should be not only a light to us, but they should also be a flame consuming the selfishness which prevents the growth of holiness. Jesus "loved us to the end," to the very limit of love: the cross. This love must come from within, from our union with Christ. It must be an outpouring of our love for God, superior and sisters in one family, a family with the common Father, who is in heaven. Loving must be as normal to us as living and breathing, day after day until our death.

• Love each other as God loves each one of you, with an intense and particular love. Be kind to each other: it is better to commit faults with gentleness than to work miracles with unkindness.

• Love begins at home, right inside our community. We cannot love outside unless we really love our brothers and sisters inside. So I say we need a very clean heart to be able to see God. When we all see God in each other, we will love one another as he loves us all. That is the fulfillment of the law, to love one another. This is all Jesus came to teach us: that God loves us, and that he wants us to love one another as he loves us.

• In order to survive, love must feed on sacrifice. Jesus' words, "Love each other as I have loved you," should not only be a light for us but also a flame to burn away our selfishness.

St. Thérèse of Lisieux used to say, "When I act and think with charity, I feel that it is Jesus who works in me. The deeper my union with him, the stronger is my love for those who live in Carmel."

• All human beings are brothers and sisters. All of us have been created by the same loving hand of God. Jesus has said to us all, "Love one another as I have loved you" (Jn 15:12). And he has also said, "As the Father has loved me, so love one another" (see John 15:9). Having this command of Jesus, we cannot be known for a party spirit.

• We must love with Jesus' love and his spirit of sacrifice. God loved us by giving himself to us. Mary loved us by sharing Jesus with us. Jesus loved us by giving up his life for us and giving his body to us as the Bread of Life. We too must give ourselves to one another. Because of this, we must reject whatever would keep us from giving ourselves to one another. We must look at it as something dangerous, something that would destroy us. I think that anything that destroys or opposes this unity cannot come from God. It comes from the devil. Just as St. Ignatius says, whatever perverts or destroys comes from the devil. The devil is the father of lies. He is capable of telling us a whole pack of lies in hopes of destroying us.

• God loves those to whom he can give more, those who expect more from him, those who are open, those who sense their need and rely on him for everything. Our works are just an expression of the growth of God's love in us. Therefore, he who is more united to God is the one who loves his neighbor more.

• Jesus says: "As the Father has loved me (by giving me to the world), I have loved you (by giving my life for you). Love as I have loved you (by giving yourself)." This giving is prayer, the sacrifice of chastity, poverty, obedience, and wholehearted, free service.

• There is no limit to God's love. It is without measure and its depth cannot be sounded. This is shown by his living and dying among us. Now turn the same picture around. There must be no limit to the love that prompts us to give ourselves to God, to be the victim of his unwanted love, that is, the love of God that has not been accepted by men.

• Love is not something that fossilizes, but something that lives. Works of love are the way to peace. And where does this love begin?—right in our hearts. We must know that we have been created for greater things, not just to be a number in the world, not just to go for diplomas and degrees, this work and that work. We have been created in order to love and to be loved.

• Jesus came into this world for one purpose. He came to give us the good news that God loves us, that God is love, that he loves you, and he loves me. He wants us to love one another as he loves each one of us.

• Our mission is to convey God's love—not a dead God but a living one.

• We read in Scripture that God speaks of his love for us, "I have loved you with an everlasting love" (Jer 31:3, RSV).

And he also says, "I have called you by your name. You are mine. The waters will not drown you. Fire will not burn you. I will give up nations for you. You are precious to me. I love you. Even if a mother could forget her child, I will not forget you. I have carved you on the palm of my hand. You are precious to me. I love you" (see Isaiah 43:1-4; 49:15-16). These are the words of God himself for you, for me, for everyone, even for the poorest of the poor.

Therefore, every time God looks at his hand, he sees me there. He sees you there too. It is something very beautiful to remember in times of suffering, loneliness, humiliation, and failure.

Remember, you are there in his hand.
You are precious to him.
He loves you.
What a truly wonderful thing!

• I will give you one more beautiful example of God's love. A man came to our house and said, "My only child is dying! The doctor has prescribed a medicine that you can get only in England." (Now I have permission from our government to store life-saving medicines that are gathered from all over the country. We have many people that go from house to house and gather leftover medicines. And they bring them to us and we give them to our poor people. We have thousands of people who come to our dispensaries.) While we were talking, a man came in with a basket of medicines.

I looked at that basket of medicines: right on the top was the very medicine that man needed for his dying child! If it had been underneath, I wouldn't have seen it.

If he had come earlier or later, I would not have remembered. He came just in time.

I stood in front of that basket and I was thinking, "There are millions of children in the world, and God is concerned with that little child in the slums of Calcutta. To send that man at that very moment! To put the medicine right on the top, so I could see it!"

See God's tender concern for you and for me! He would do the same thing for each one of you.

• We should gather to give thanks to God for what he has done in us, with us, and through us. We thank him for having used you and us to be his love and mercy. God is still love, and he still loves the world. We believe that God so loved the world that he gave his only begotten Son. And God so loves the world today that he gives you and me to love the world, so that we may be his love and his mercy.

What a beautiful thought and conviction for us, that we can be that love and mercy right in our homes, above all. Then we can be that love and mercy for our next-door neighbors and for our neighbors down the street.

• Jesus has chosen us for himself. We belong to him. Let us be so convinced of this "belonging" that we allow nothing, however small, to separate us from his love.

• This is the only condition that Christ really places on us: "Love one another as I have loved you." And we know very well how much he has loved us! He died for us!

• I will tell you another good example of how generous and great our people are.

We had picked up a young orphan boy whose mother had died in the home for dying destitutes. She had come from a good family, but had come down in life because of difficult circumstances.

The boy grew up and wanted to become a priest. When he was asked, "Why do you want to become a priest?" he gave a very simple answer. "I want to do for other children what Mother Teresa has done for me. I want to love as she loved me. I want to serve as she served me."

Today he is a priest, devoted to loving all those who have nothing and no one—those who have forgotten what human love is, or the warmth of a human touch, or even the kindness of a smile.

*By this all men will know that you are my disciples,*
*if you have love for one another.*

• May the love of Christ be a living bond between every two of us. From that others will realize that we are true Missionaries of Charity.

• In 1973 I accompanied my sisters to Ethiopia. The emperor asked me, "What are the sisters going to do here? What can they accomplish?"

I answered, "They will offer your people the love and kindness of Jesus."

He replied, "This is something new, a new coming of Christ."

• We should make a decision to do little things with great love. When Thérèse of Lisieux—the Little Flower—died and was about to be canonized, everyone was asking, "What reason is there for the Holy Father to canonize her? She hasn't done anything extraordinary." The Holy Father pointed out in writing the reason for his decision: "I want to canonize her because she did ordinary things with extraordinary love."

• This is one of the things that most impresses me. Wherever I go, I always hear about Co-workers who love one another in such a way that no one is able to sow disunity in their midst. There is a oneness of spirit and soul that binds them together, so that their oneness is unaffected even if they are sometimes far away from each other. This harmony is something that you must guard carefully. Don't let anything come between you and your co-worker or threaten your harmony. If such a thing should happen, you will be Co-workers in name only and not from the heart.

• The first Christians died willingly for Jesus, and they were known for their love for one another. Never has the world had a greater need for love than in our day. People are hungry for love.

• Some time ago a Hindu gentleman was asked, "What is a Christian?" He gave an answer that was both very simple and surprising. "A Christian is someone who gives of himself."

• To make it easier for us to love each other, Jesus has told us, "Whatever you do for the least of my brethren, you do it to me. When you receive a child in my name, you are receiving me" (see Luke 9:48). "When you give a glass of water to somebody in my name, you give it to me" (see Mark 9:41).

This is the love Jesus has brought to earth.

This is the love we must show to each other.

Why? Because he loved us first.

"Precisely because of the love that you will have for each other, they will recognize that you are my disciples, that you are Christians" (see John 13:35).

• Christ uses me as an instrument to put you in touch with his poor. This is what I think happens when I go wherever I am called: many people are joined together by the sense of the common need for God.

• The unity of Christians is an important thing because Christians are a light for others. If we are Christians, we must look like Christ—this is my deep conviction.

• Each time anyone comes in contact with us, they must become different and better people because of having met us. We must radiate God's love.

• Our brothers and sisters are found scattered around the world. It is wonderful to see how people welcome us, to hear them exclaim, "The sisters and brothers are Christ's love among us." Remember me telling you how the sisters arrived in the Muslim country of Yemen. It was the first time in eight hundred years that a Catholic sister had been seen in that country. The head of the government of that country wrote to a priest in Rome, saying, "The sisters' presence has kindled a new light in the lives of our people." The sisters are not called Missionaries of Charity there. They are called the "Carriers of God's Love."

*Something Beautiful for God*

Come with me into a world of poverty,
Into a land where men are dying endlessly,
Into a world of inhumanity.
Can't you see they're starving, where's your charity?
They laugh and cry, they're people just like you and me,
They need help and not just sympathy.

Chorus:
Show each one something beautiful for God above,
Something beautiful to show your love,
Something beautiful for God above,
Something beautiful to show your love.

A day goes by, the night is long for everyone.
A child is crying, perhaps he'll live to see the sun,
And yet he knows the morning may not come.
Throughout the world our brothers live in poverty,
They're everywhere, if only we have eyes to see,
So look around and find your sanity.
Show to men the love that he has shown to you,
And feed his lambs as he has fed each one of you,
He loves them as much as he loves you.